RIDE

23 GREAT MOTORCYCLE RIDES IN THE NORTH STAR STATE

MINNESOTA

Cynthia Lueck Sowden

Table of Contents

For Ralph, who takes me on all his adventures.

Foreword

With many of its roads laid out in a strict, Midwest-grid pattern, Minnesota does not, at first glance, appear to be a motorcyclist's paradise. While you won't encounter the soaring mountains and the hairpin turns of Colorado's "Million Dollar Highway," you can find plenty of fun riding along the lakes and rivers, over the bluffs, and through the prairies.

My husband Ralph and I got the idea for this book after taking a 4,400-mile trip to the Grand Canyon and back on his 2002 Victory. The following summer, gas prices shot up to nearly $4 per gallon, and we decided to see what we could see in our home state. This book is the culmination of a couple of summers of motorcycling through the North Star State. We have circumnavigated the state, and set foot in all four corners.

Ralph and I had fun researching the book. He did the driving, and I rode pillion, gawked, and took photos on the fly. At rest stops, I furiously wrote down all my impressions before they faded away. I re-traced our routes several times and wore holes in my Minnesota highway map.

Not all of the roads we traveled are mentioned in this book. The Waters of the Dancing Sky Byway in northern Minnesota, for example, has been omitted. The highway, also known as MN 11, runs straight across the top of the state from International Falls to Baudette. While it may be a great place to see the Northern Lights, it's flat, there are few curves, and the scenery consists primarily of tamarack and alder swamps. Definitely not a biker's road!

We reported road conditions as we found them. They may have changed—for better or for worse–since we passed over them. (Some rural roads are just plain awful. If Minnesota motorcyclists banded together to take a legislator for a ride, maybe some of our roads would receive better attention!)

About Our Bike

Our 2002 Victory Cruiser

Ralph's motorcycle is a champagne-and cream 1508cc 2002 Victory Deluxe Touring Cruiser. We purchased it secondhand from a guy who said it had been made for one the executives at Polaris. It had just 3,000 miles on it. We have added 30,000 to the total. It's a very comfortable bike. Ralph has added true dual ceramic coated pipes because, he says, it gives him better performance and gas mileage. I think he just likes to make noise.

How to Use This Book

This book is part road map/part travelogue. I've tried to make it an interactive experience for those with e-readers. You'll find website links scattered throughout the text. Follow them to get an idea of what you'll be seeing. If you're carrying a printed book with you, we've provided quick route directions at the top of each "ride" so you don't have to search for turns in the text.

Maps

The maps in this book are not intended for navigational use but to give you a sense of routes and where they are in the state. Many bikers have GPS systems and can use them to get from point A to point B. The State of Minnesota still publishes highway maps. You can order one free of charge at www.exploreminnesota.com.

Naming Conventions

I started out naming the roads in a very literary fashion, i.e., U.S. Hwy. 169, Minnesota Hwy. 12. This became very cumbersome as I wrote, so I standardized them to US 169 or MN 12.

Distances

Distances between places are approximate and were calculated according to Google maps. We tried to cover three or four rides per trip, so our actual mileage was much greater than the rides described in this book. We did not take strict odometer readings at the beginning and ending of each ride but at the beginning and ending of each trip.

I also found Google's aerial views helpful in locating things I saw along the way and keeping them "in order of appearance" along the road.

Another valuable resource was the third edition of Warren Upham's *Minnesota Place Names* (Minnesota Historical Society Press, 2001), which provided interesting tidbits of history as well as the origins of the names of cities, towns, rivers and lakes.

We hope our "finds" inspire you to take a motorcycle tour yourself. As the Minnesota Department of Tourism says, "Explore Minnesota!"

Cynthia Lueck Sowden
January 2013

Rules of the Road

Minnesota Motorcycle Regulations

Despite its reputation as a "nanny" state, Minnesota has surprisingly few rules when it comes down to motorcycles. Normal traffic rules apply, of course. There are some special regulations for motorcycles and motorcyclists, most of them concerned with safety.

- If you're a Minnesota licensed driver, you must have a motorcycle endorsement on your license to legally operate a motorcycle in the state. To obtain an endorsement, you need to get an instruction permit. Permits are issued at driver examination stations after you pass a written knowledge test about motorcycles.
- If you're riding a motorcycle with an instruction permit,

  - You must wear a federal Department of Transportation-approved helmet and eye protection
  - You may not carry passengers
  - You may not ride on Interstate highways
  - You may not ride at night

- After you get the permit, you can obtain an endorsement by taking a motorcycle skills test. You can schedule one in person, by phone or online at www.mndriverinfo.org. Endorsements are $13 and are renewed when you renew your driver's license.
- All motorcycles must be registered with the state and show a license plate that proves the registration tax has been paid. All motorcycle registrations expire in February and must be renewed each year. If you're new to the state, you have 60 days to register your bike.
- Motorcycles registered in Minnesota must have liability insurance for property damage or injury to another party.

The Minnesota Department of Public Safety publishes a 66-page *Motorcycle, Motorized Bicycle and Electric-assisted Bicycle Manual,* which offers a lot of useful information about riding a motorcycle, as well as basic rules for riders. It's available free at state Drivers License Exam stations, or you can download a copy from http://www.dps.state.mn.us/dvs/DLTraining/DLManual/MotorcycleManual.htm

Other Road Rules

These rules are just plain common sense:

- The motorcycle driver's seat must be permanently mounted to the bike.
- Passengers may ride only on a permanent, regular passenger's seat or sidecar.
- Passengers must be able to reach the footrests on both sides of the bike. That pretty much means no kids on the back.

- Drivers and passengers must sit facing forward, astride the motorcycle, unless the passenger is in a sidecar.
- Bundles should be secured to the backrest or in saddle bags. Don't try to drive and hold on to your groceries at the same time.
- Do not ride between lanes. You can split the lanes in California, but you can't do it here.
- The bike's headlight should be on at all times.

Then there's the "undetected vehicle" law. This 2002 Minnesota law allows you to drive against a red light, and is based on five conditions:

- The motorcycle has been brought to a complete stop.
- The traffic-control signal continues to beam red, even though you've been sitting there for a long time.
- The semaphore isn't working, or has been programmed to change to green only after it detects a vehicle—and you haven't been detected.
- No other vehicles or persons are on the roadway you want to cross or enter.
- Approaching vehicles or persons are so far away they don't present a problem.

Street Legal

In Minnesota, a properly-equipped motorcycle should have

- A rearview mirror, horn and muffler.
- One, but not more than two, headlights with high- and low-beam settings. Headlight modulators are okay.

- One red taillight, including a brake light. You can have a blue dot up to one inch in diameter on the taillight.
- Footrests for your passenger.
- One brake, front or rear, operated by hand or foot.
- The driver's seat should be permanent.
- Passengers may ride only on a permanent seat or in a sidecar.

Your Gear

A medieval knight would never think of entering the jousting ring without his armor and chain mail. Yet it's not uncommon to see sun-starved Minnesotans racing along city streets in tank tops, shorts and tennis shoes. Nearly 80 percent of motorcycle crashes result in death or injury.[1] Although it's tempting to leave them home on a warm day, we try to make wearing our leathers a habit, even on a 105-degree day in Winona! Whether it's a long ride or a short one, leathers are still your best protection.

Helmets are an even bigger lifesaver. Ralph once lost control of his bike on I-35W at the eastbound I-94 split. He slid on his face and chest for several feet and woke up in an ambulance. If not for his helmet, he would not have lived to help me research this book.

Minnesota does not require licensed riders to use helmets. If, however, you are under 18 years old or are operating under a learner's permit, you must wear a DOT-approved helmet. Whatever your status, the helmet will do you more good on your head than it will on the back of your bike.

---

1   *Minnesota Motorcycle, Motorized Bicycle and Electric-Assisted Bicycle Manual*, Minnesota Department of Public Safety

Ralph's helmet and jacket after a close encounter with I-35W.

You can make yourself, your helmet or your bike more visible with retroreflective decals. Free decals are available from the Minnesota Department of Public Safety. Just send a self-addressed, stamped envelope to

MMSC Reflective Decal
Minnesota Department of Public Safety
444 Cedar Street, Suite 155
St. Paul, MN 55101

Minnesota requires riders to wear some form of protective eyewear, even if your motorcycle has a windscreen. Glasses and goggles are good; a full-face helmet is even better at keeping insects and gravel out of your eyes. Sorry, contact lenses don't qualify.

Weather

In general, the motorcycle season in Minnesota runs from April through October. At roughly the same latitude as Siberia, the state also experiences the same extremes in weather. One year riders braved an April snowstorm to participate in the annual Flood Run. The following year Ralph and I took a ride up to Pequot Lakes on St. Patrick's Day (March 17). It was a balmy 60 degrees, and the high school bands paraded in their shirtsleeves, even though ice still covered the lakes.

Thunderstorm near Pipestone

If you're headed out for an extended cruise, be sure to check the weather. With an "eye on the sky," you may be able to make adjustments to your route and avoid bad weather. It's not unusual for a summer thunderstorm to roll up just in time for the evening rush hour or to see snowflakes swirl during an October ride.

Temperatures easily climb or fall 30 degrees in a day, sometimes in a matter of minutes.

Be sure to pack accordingly. Leathers do a great job of blocking out the wind. A rain suit can feel good during a summer storm or on a misty fall day. Long underwear is also nice to have on hand during spring and autumn rides. You can always take it off as the day warms up.

Rule Number One for riding in Minnesota weather: If in doubt, don't ride.

Minnesota's "Other Season": Road Construction

Road construction on MN 11

The joke among native Minnesotans is that there are two seasons, winter and road construction. It's not uncommon to find your route narrowed to a single lane or blocked by orange barricades with signs that instruct you to go elsewhere. Check www.511mn.org for up-to-date road conditions.

Wildlife

Minnesota has an abundance of deer. If you think a car-deer collision is messy, a motorcycle-deer collision can be downright disastrous. Deer like to travel along the edges of fields and roads. Keep an eye out for these hoofed creatures, especially during the half-light of dawn or dusk. They can't tell time, however, so they don't always abide by this rule. On a trip to International Falls Ralph and I saw three deer at three different places within a space of a half-hour, around 10:00 a.m. Each was about to cross the road—and into our path–in broad daylight. Our Victory's loud pipes came in handy; a couple of snorts on the throttle sent them back into hiding.

If you're traveling in northeastern Minnesota, you may have a similar experience with moose. You'll find them in swampy areas, and you're most apt to encounter them during dawn or dusk.

Skunks, raccoons, porcupines and opossums are nocturnal animals. You're not likely to encounter them unless you have a penchant for riding in rural areas at night. However, you may have to dodge their carcasses in daylight. Skunks and coons are distributed statewide; porcupines are found in the north; possums are mostly like to be found in the southeastern part of the state.

Wild turkeys are another hazard. They've been known to fly up from the roadside and through car windshields. They're hefty birds and could do some serious damage to a bike. Be on the alert for them in open fields, particularly in southern Minnesota.

Before You Go

Maybe you've heard the expression, "There are old pilots and bold pilots, but there are no old, bold pilots." The same is true for motorcyclists. Take a tip from veteran airplane pilots and perform a complete walk-around inspection before you head out on the highway. The Minnesota Motorcycle Safety Foundation has devised a "T-CLOCS" system[2]:

Tires and Wheels

- Make sure the front and rear brakes work properly and feel firm.
- Make sure your tire pressure is at the level recommended by the motorcycle manufacturer.

Controls

- Try the clutch and throttle, and make sure they operate smoothly.
- Test the horn.
- Adjust your mirrors, and make sure they're clean.

---

2   A copy of the TCLOCS checklist is in the back of the *Minnesota Motorcycle, Motorized Bicycle and Electric-Assisted Bicycle Manual.* It's a good thing to keep handy with your bike.

Lights

- Check your headlight and taillight. Make sure your high and low beams work.
- Test the left and right turn signal lights.
- Be sure the brake light lights when you apply the front or back brakes.

Oil and Fluids

- Look under the bike to make sure it's not leaking oil.
- Check the brake hydraulic fluid and the coolant level.
- Check the engine oil and transmission fluid levels. If you're on a long trip, take an extra quart of oil with you.
- Be sure the fuel valve is open before you start your engine.

Chassis

- Make sure the chain or belt is adjusted to manufacturer's specifications.
- Make sure the front suspension doesn't bind and that rear shocks and springs move smoothly.

Stands

Be certain the kickstand operates smoothly and folds up tightly against the bike when you're riding.

If you have someone else work on your bike, double-check their work. One summer Ralph and I took a vacation to the Grand Canyon, following Route 66 from Oklahoma to Arizona. Before leaving Minnesota, he took the bike to a local dealer for an oil change and new tires because he was busy at work and didn't have the time to do it himself.

On a side trip up the mountains near Sedona, Ariz., the motorcycle began making odd clunking noises and jerking motions—a very uncomfortable feeling when you're going up the middle of a switchback! Fortunately, we made it to the Victory dealer in Flagstaff. The mechanic there discovered that the drive train belt was loose, causing the rear axle to wobble. Thinking it was about time to change the oil, Ralph asked the mechanic to do so. That was when we found out that the washer holding the oil plug was the wrong size and was leaking.

When it comes to riding a motorcycle, you can never be too careful.

Travel Tips

Money-saving Ideas for Motorcyclists

Thank God, motorcycles don't burn a lot of gas. But, while the price of gas will never be under your control, you can lower some of your travel expenses.

State Park Permits

If you plan to visit more than one of Minnesota's 66 state parks, save some money by purchasing a motorcycle permit. They're $20, and they give you year-round admission into all the parks plus six recreation areas. You can keep the permit in your billfold. At this time, park permits are sold only at state parks.

If you'd like to stay in the state parks, it's a good idea to make reservations, especially for the most popular parks, including Itasca. Only 30 percent of the campsites are available on a first-come, first-served basis. Go to http://www.dnr.state.mn.us/state_parks/reservations.html. Choose the park and choose your accommodations—some parks offer camper cabins that sleep up to six people, others have only campsites. Reservations are good up to a year in advance.

Minnesota Historical Society Membership

If you enjoy seeing history come to life, the Minnesota Historical Society does it well. The Society operates 26 historic sites throughout the state. Membership gives you free admission to all of them, plus free admission to museums across the nation that participate in the Time Traveler program, and a subscription to *Minnesota History* magazine. See http://www.mnhs.org for sites, membership details and upcoming events.

AAA of Minnesota

AAA members get a discount at participating hotels and motels. Just show your membership card at check-in. AAA members can also get discounts on theater tickets, at restaurants and amusement parks and service at AAA-member garages. That's worth the price of membership, even if you don't have them plan your trip! (Note: AAA discounts and benefits are available throughout the U.S.)

Minnesota Department of Tourism

You can get lots of free travel advice and information from the state's tourism folks as well as official Minnesota roadmaps and a yearly travel guide. Visit http://www.exploreminnesota.com. You'll also find a "Deals" section on the website with special rates for wine tours, B&Bs, golf and a number of other activities.

Foreign Travel: Bring your passport

If you're in the northern reaches of the state and have a hankering to visit Canada, make sure you bring your passport. Border security has tightened since 9/11/2001, and you'll need to prove your U.S. citizenship when you return to Minnesota.

Stay Hydrated

This applies to you *and* your bike. We found that motorcycle riding is thirsty work, so we began carrying refillable stainless steel water bottles in our saddle bags. A sip of water kept us going a little longer, especially on hot days.

Checking the price of gas in Paynesville

Be aware that the farther north you go in Minnesota, the fewer people you'll see. Fewer people mean fewer towns and fewer gas stations. In northwestern Minnesota in particular, you may think you are the last person on earth! Keep an eye on the gas tank and fill it often.

The Northwest

Prairies, Lakes and Sky

When the glaciers retreated from this part of Minnesota, they scoured the land, leaving broad, flat prairies and lakes and potholes galore. Though less "wild" than northeastern Minnesota, there are plenty of hills and curves to take, and places to feel the sun on your face and freedom in the air.

The King of Trails, US 75

Noyes to Breckenridge, 206 miles

*Since we'd already traveled US 75 from Luverne to Ortonville,
we just had to see the northern half of the ride!*

We were alone on the highway on our way to Noyes. We
were flying along US 75, not far from the Canadian border.
Suddenly, a bright yellow airplane dipped out of the blue,
cloudless sky. It was a Pacer Cub, the kind Ralph's father, Joe,
used to fly. The pilot swooped down low over us, as if to get a
closer look, then shot skyward again. At lunch, we laughed and

decided that it *was* Joe, "buzzing" us and wishing us well from heaven.

That plane was the only vehicle we encountered on our way to a place that used to be a U. S. border station and now is nearly a ghost town. Ralph had become fascinated with Noyes (pronounced "noise") during the week before we decided to ride across the top of the state and down its western border.

Back in the days when oxcarts hauled goods from Canada into Minnesota, Noyes was an important border crossing. Later on, trains stopped there, and the town was named after the station master, J.A. Noyes. Use of the border station declined after I-29 was built in North Dakota. The Canadian town of Emerson, Manitoba, shut down its port of entry in 2003; the U. S. government followed suit and closed Noyes in 2006.

The empty customs station at Noyes

The customs building sits empty. The outdoor ashtrays still stand sentry duty next to the front doors, which sport a large Department of Homeland Security sticker. Through the plate-glass windows, we could see a wastebasket in the hallway. The barricade to the border is down, its lights still flash a warning. On the Canadian side of the border, weeds grow up through the cracked concrete of the unused road.

There are a couple of occupied homes in Noyes. The rest stare blindly at Hwy. 75. After checking out the international boundary marker, we turned the motorcycle south and began to explore the King of Trails from the top of the state down.

Land in the Red River Valley is flat and seemingly endless. Trees, when they're present, are lined up in shelter belts planted after the drought and Dust Bowl years of the 1930s. Their straight rows divide acres and acres of ruffly-leaved sugar beets, the area's predominant crop.

From Noyes, we passed through St. Vincent Junction, Humboldt and Hallock, the seat of Kittson County. As we followed US 75 through Hallock, the gaudy colors of the Gateway Motel and Museum caught my eye. What's in the museum? According to the Explore Minnesota website, toys and autos. Once on the road, however, we keep moving. We rode on past the museum and the grain elevator and on through the towns of Kennedy and Donaldson.

At Argyle, a large sign informed us that the Stephen-Argyle Central football team was the 2009 winner of the State Nine-man football championship.

The blacktop from Noyes to Warren is good. From Warren to Crookston, it's one bump after another. We bumped and jostled through Angus and Euclid. It's a land of few people and fewer gas stations.

As we approached Crookston, the fields of sugar beets were interspersed with acres of sunflowers insistently showing their faces to the sun, and soybeans and wheat. Crookston is home to one of the University of Minnesota's Ag Experiment Stations and it's one of the U's smaller campuses with average enrollment of 1,400 students.

As you near the campus, Hwy. 75 runs concurrently with US 2. The two highways become a four-lane road known locally as University Ave. At W. 6th St., the highways take a bend to the left. In four blocks they take a right and become a one-way street heading south at Main St.

The Red Lake River squiggles its way through Crookston. You'll cross it as you ride along Main St. There's a wildflower garden on the corner across from the Crookston Fire Department. It's tended by the General Federation of Women's Club of Crookston, an international organization that has conservation and beautification as its goals.

Hwy. 75 swings to the west, passing the American Crystal Sugar plant on the south side of town. The cooperative is a big presence in Crookston. August is the beginning of the harvest season for the long, tan sugar beets, and we passed a number of semis filled with them on their way to the sugar plant.

As it leaves Crookston, US 75 begins a series of long curves and angles southwest toward the Minnesota-North Dakota border before starting a fairly straight run to Fargo-Moorhead. We crossed the Sand Hill River into the town of Climax, named for a long-ago barnside ad for Climax Tobacco.

Wayside rests along the highway are in short supply. We pulled off in the little town of Shelly and found a nice city park to stretch our legs and enjoy our picnic lunch.

At Hendrum a local wit has posted a sign, "Hendrum Next 9 Exits"– for the nine intersections that cross US 75 and make up the entire town.

Perley, Georgetown and Kragnes were a blur as we sped through. US 75 curves slightly toward each these little towns, as if it hates to pass them by.

In Moorhead we slowed down to the requisite 30 miles per hour. The highway brings you straight into the city, past the Moorhead softball diamonds. It takes a left at Center Ave., where it joins US 10 and runs for about a mile. At Eighth St., US 75 takes a left and passes by Concordia College. There are a number of hotels along this street, if you're looking for a place to stay the night.

The Comstock House sits at 506 S. 8th St. It's the home of Solomon Comstock, who started the First National Bank and Moorhead University and helped James J. Hill establish his railroad in the area. Ada Comstock was the first dean of women at the University of Minnesota and president of Radcliffe College. The house is open for tours weekends from Memorial Day to Labor Day.

From Moorhead to Breckenridge, US 75 stays close to the Red River of the North. Sunlight bounced off the water and flashed through the trees on the river's banks. As we crossed over the Whiskey River near Kent, I was struck by the cloudiness of the water. It looked almost gray.

The Red River was on our right as we rolled into Breckenridge. We ended our Red River Valley excursion by looking for a place to stay.

Minnesota Hwy. 9

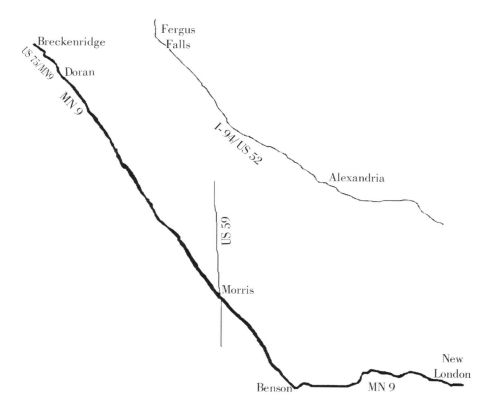

Breckenridge to New London, 103 miles

This ride offers very little traffic and, as you enter the Glacial Ridge area, lots of hills and curves.

Minnesota 9 is part of the International Prairie Passage, a scenic drive that stretches from Texas to Manitoba, and the Glacial Ridge Trail Scenic Byway, which is unique to Minnesota. The Prairie Passage is designated by a sign illustrated by with two yellow coneflowers. The Glacial Ridge is marked with a black arrowhead outlined in red and pointing downward.

The ride begins in Breckenridge,[3] which shares the distinction of being at the head of the Red River Valley of the North with its across-the-river neighbor, Wahpeton, N.D. The headwaters are formed by the meeting of the Otter Tail and Bois de Sioux rivers. A granite marker along the riverfront in Headwaters Park maps the Red's route to Winnipeg, Manitoba.

Catch 9 at the corner of Minnesota Ave.e and 5th St. N. Drive south. At this point, MN 9 runs concurrently with US 75. Fifth St. bends to the left and becomes Buffalo Ave. On the right side of the road is a farm implement dealer whose parking lot is lined with several humongous John Deere combines. Clearly, he's banking on a good sugar beet harvest to have so much green on display.

And this is sugar beet country. The terrain is incredibly flat, and rows of sugar beets stretch to the horizon, interrupted only by farmstead shelter belts. If you look carefully along this section

---

3 Hwy. 9 actually begins in Crookston.

of the Prairie Passage, you may spot prickly pear cactus growing in the ditches.

East of Breckenridge the road bends to the southeast. There are some nice curves as you approach the town of Doran, where US 75 and MN 9 split. From Doran to Morris the pavement is extremely rough, and you have to watch so that your wheels don't catch in the ruts in the middle of the lane. The gravel shoulders are narrow. A railroad line keeps pace with you on the right. In between is a wide right-of-way that's populated with telephone poles that are either the shortest ever made or are sunk very deeply into the earth.

You may see pelicans overhead as you skirt Doran and Campbell or snowy egrets wading in the shallow waters of prairie potholes and ditches. You'll cross the Rabbit River at Campbell. It's a brown little stream, not very wide.

As you cross MN 55, you'll leave Wilkin County and breeze through the northeast corner of Traverse County and the little town of Tintah (Dakota for "prairie") before entering Grant County just south of Charlesville.

The towns along this portion of the route were once lively farm communities. Now they are bedroom communities for larger towns and they hold empty reminders of gas stations, storefronts and grain elevators. All that's left of the co-op station at Norcross, for example, is a line of empty gas pumps.

At Norcross you'll cross the Mustinka River (from the Dakota word, *mashtincha*, or rabbit. There must have been a lot of bunnies in this area.). The Mustinka used to follow a more winding course, but it has been straightened and channeled into submission (it's even known as State Ditch No. 19!). It flows into Lake Traverse on the state's western edge.

You'll pass by several small lakes near Herman, just a few miles north of the Stevens County line. The road improves as you roll into Morris, home of the <u>University of Minnesota's</u> third college campus. It's an orderly town with establishments that cater to a young college crowd.

If you're looking for a place for a quick breakfast or lunch, stop in at DeToy's at 802 Atlantic Ave. This family-owned restaurant stakes its claim on its chicken—"If the Colonel had our recipe, he'd be a general"—and doesn't stint on its breakfast sausage or ham. Expect generous portions and friendly service.

Back on the road, MN 9 is in good shape from Morris to Benson. It's here that the highway makes a turn to the east, away from the prairie, and into the Glacial Ridge area of Minnesota.

The <u>Glacial Ridge</u> was created 30,000 years ago during the last Ice Age. As the glacier retreated, it left behind an area of lakes and hills that looks like a rumpled blue and green patchwork quilt. It's a fun area for motorcycling, with S-curves, curvy hills and scenic vistas seemingly everywhere you look. None of the curves are difficult, nor are the hills steep; all of them are pleasurable. The route becomes almost squiggly!

You'll enter Kandiyohi County just before Sunberg. As you near the town, you'll see a sign for MN 104. If you make a right turn, you'll drive down a gravel road to <u>Monson Lake State Park</u>, known for its walleye fishing and bird-watching. You'll pass by Games Lake and Swan Lake; their refreshing waters look ever-so inviting. Closer to New London, you'll see signs for 2,500-acre <u>Sibley State Park</u>, named for Civil War hero and Minnesota's first governor, Henry Hastings Sibley. You can get a 360-degree view of the area at the observation tower on Mt. Tom, inside the park.

It's a curvy, downhill roll into New London where MN 9 ends at the junction with MN 23. There are several gift shops in the area and the region is filled with resorts where you can kick back and waterski, fish or swim. If you're there during the second week of August, you may catch the start of the annual New London to New Brighton Antique Car Run, patterned after the London to Brighton Car Run in England.

This cute little town could be the end of your journey, or just a pause. A few miles south on MN 23 is Spicer. Take a cruise around Green Lake, lined with beautiful lake homes. Then catch Kandiyohi Co. 10 and follow the Crow River toward the Twin Cities. There are plenty of hills and curves out there—just pick a road and find them!

Best Steak!

If you're staying in the Breckenridge area, drive across the Red River to Wahpeton, N.D., for an excellent meal. Head west on Minnesota Avenue (it becomes Dakota Avenue as you cross the bridge, and the state line).Continue to 11th Street N., and take a right. Drive north to the corner of 16th and 11th, where you'll find Prante's Fine Dining. Although it's a white table-cloth restaurant, they also serve dinner in the bar. And what a dinner! The steaks are nicely seasoned, extremely tender, and grilled to perfection. They also serve humongous pork chops, seafood and pasta. Dinner for two—including dessert—is about $50.

Minnesota Hwy. 210 East

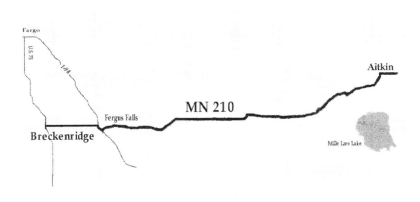

Breckenridge to Aitkin, 158 miles

From one lake-spattered region to another, it's a pretty ride.

When you look at a map of Minnesota, the areas around Fergus Falls and Brainerd look as though someone had shaken a paintbrush, a la Jackson Pollock, and spattered blue paint on the canvas. Those blue spatters are lakes, hundreds of them, left behind in the wake of the glaciers that once covered the state. This ride takes you past some of those lakes as it brings you from the western to the north central part of the state.

Pick up MN 210 at its intersection with US 75 in Breckenridge. If you're coming from the north, the two highways run together just as you approach St. Francis Medical Center. If you're coming from the south, US 75 and MN 210 meet at Wilkin Co. 9. In either case, go east.

As you leave the city, the land rises. You're leaving the Red River Valley and its fertile fields behind. The road is straight, the pavement good on this two-lane highway. You'll pass through the Agassiz Waterfowl Production Area, managed by the U.S. Fish and Wildlife Service. Despite its industrial-sounding name, the area encompasses 679 acres of native tallgrass prairie. If you're a bird-watcher, look for American bittern, greater prairie-chicken, sedge wren, common yellowthroat, clay-colored, savannah and swamp sparrows, bobolink and American goldfinch.

Trees become more numerous as you near Fergus Falls, and the road begins to curve. Farms look like miniature industrial complexes, each surrounded by several buildings, lines of planting and harvesting equipment, and grain bins and dryers.

As you touch Fergus Falls' western edge, the highway wants to divert you around the city via I-94. It's a short diversion, but if you're a purist, you can ride MN 210 into downtown Fergus. The main drag, Lincoln Ave., is actually part of 210.

Lincoln Ave. takes you through the city's stately and well-preserved downtown. As West Lincoln becomes East Lincoln and curves to the south to become S. Sheridan St., you'll pass the Riverside Waterfowl Sanctuary, one of the top bird-watching sites in the state. The Otter Tail River provides habitat for Canada geese, mallard, wood and ring-neck ducks and trumpeter swans. Swans are most apt to be in the vicinity in the winter, but you may catch glimpses of them in spring or autumn.

At the corner of Sheridan and E. Vernon Ave., turn to the left. E. Vernon becomes Pebble Lake Rd. before it connects with the main 210 artery once more southeast of Fergus Falls.

If you follow the I-94 diversion, you'll find that the freeway is concurrent with US 59. Merge onto I-94 and follow it for about three and a half miles to Exit 57/Otter Tail Co. 25. Take a left onto 25. This is also known as S. Cascade St. and the MN 210 Bypass. The bypass leads you to the Pebble Lake Rd. intersection. Continue heading east on MN 210.

You'll pass a number of small lakes before reaching the north side of 683-acre Wall Lake. On a map, the lake looks like a question mark in the middle of the prairie. The highway curves around it before sending you on to Underwood. With a total area of .4 mile, you're in one side of Underwood and out the other, just long enough to read the billboard and learn that the local school team is called the Rockets. Heading east from Underwood, the highway takes a dip to the south to go around South Turtle Lake. This part of the highway is also called Greenwood Trail.

Wall Lake, east of Fergus Falls

The distance between Underwood and Battle Lake is just shy of nine miles. In 1795 the area around Battle Lake was the scene of a fierce fight between fifty Ojibwe from Leech Lake and a greater number of Dakota. More than thirty Ojibwe died during the conflict. The city of Battle Lake is wrapped around the western shore of West Battle Lake.

As you leave Battle Lake, MN 210 is sandwiched between West Battle Lake and Clitherall Lake. Clitherall Lake is named after Major George Clitherall, U.S. land agent in Otter Tail County from 1858 to 1861. He gave the Minnesota Historical Society a carved mahogany armchair that once belonged to George Washington.

MN 210 turns northeastward toward Henning. Henning began its life as East Battle Lake, but the name was changed in the 1880s. It's almost a straight shot from Henning to Hewitt, but, as you enter Todd County, you're taken on a pleasant little carnival ride past numerous marshes. It's also ten miles of rough road. Wild turkeys peck at grain in the fields. The lakes diminish in number, and the landscape becomes drier.

MN 210 turns to the northeast again toward Staples where it meets with US 10 and takes a right. The two highways run together for approximately seven miles, becoming a split four-lane highway on the outskirts of town. The two become one again in Motley. As you pass the Motley City Hall, 210 splits off to the north, and US 10 heads south toward the Twin Cities. The bridge carries you across the Crow Wing River. In less than a mile, you'll cross the much smaller Mosquito River.

The highway makes two small corrections toward the south before it enters Pillager. The town gets its name from an incident in the 1760s when a trading post at the mouth of the Crow Wing River was robbed by Ojibwe from the Leech Lake area. MN 210 remains parallel with the Crow Wing as it skirts around the Camp Ripley Military Reservation and enters the Cuyuna Range.

The Cuyuna Range is an iron range discovered in 1895 by Cuyler Adams who found traces of magnetic ore in the area. It's named after him and his dog, Una. The range runs roughly from Brainerd to Aitkin and was actively mined until the 1980s. Many of the abandoned mine pits have become lakes. You can discover what the iron miners left behind at Cuyuna Country State Recreational Area near Crosby. Your Minnesota State Park permit gains you admission.

Traffic gets heavier as you near Brainerd/Baxter. In fact, the intersection of MN 210 and MN 371 can usually be counted upon to be stop-and-go, particularly on weekends. Cross the Mississippi River into Brainerd, and continue to follow 210 northeast toward the Brainerd-Crow Wing County Airport.

The two-lane highway is in good repair here, and the gentle curves bring you smoothly into Ironton, and then Crosby. If you like antiques, Crosby's main drag is lined with stores offering everything from furniture to fine china. The road brings you right down to the shores of Serpent Lake where a dragon-like serpent rises out of the water.

Continue eastward around the lake. MN 210 is also named MN 6 at this point, and it hugs Serpent Lake all the way into Deerwood. When you appear to run out of road, take a left onto 210. A large, leaping deer statue will greet you as you exit Deerwood and travel on toward Aitkin.

The Cayuna Country Club lies on the outskirts of Deerwood. It's a par 72 course with hills that make golfing interesting, if not challenging.

MN 210 winds by several lakes, some of which are visible from the highway: Rushmeyer, Casey, Cedar, Poor Farm, Dogfish, Bass and Pickerel. Farm implement dealerships populate both sides of the road as you roll into Aitkin on Second St. The Aitkin County courthouse and Aitkin High School sit kitty-corner from each other as you head toward the middle of town.

If you have time, stop at the Jacques Art Center, 121 Second St. N.W. It showcases the work of local artists as well as that of Francis Lee Jacques, who with his wife, Florence Page Jacques, authored *Snow Shoe Country* and *Canoe Country*. The museum is open from 11:00 a.m. to 4:00 p.m., Tuesday through Saturday, and admission is free.

The highway will continue to head northeastward toward Duluth, but at this time, you'll be content to stop at the intersection of MN 210 and US 169, the site of the only stoplight in Aitkin County.

The Northeast

Woods, Water and a Seacoast

Is there a more fabled part of Minnesota? Probably not. With its tall evergreens and thousands of lakes, the northeastern part of the state offers up ride after scenic ride. Throw in Lake Superior's vast expanse and rocky shores and you have Minnesota's version of the New England coast. Why wouldn't you ride there?

Edge of the Wilderness National Scenic Byway (MN 38 North)

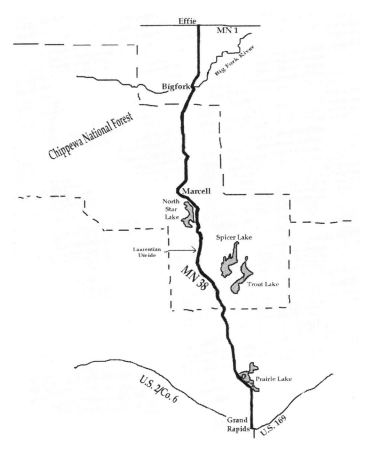

Grand Rapids to Effie, 47 miles

Don't let the slow start fool you. This is one of the best rides in Minnesota!

This ride begins in downtown Grand Rapids and ends in the small town of Effie. In between are lakes (more than 1,100 in the area!), hills and curves in abundance.

The byway was designated a national byway in 1996. There are 14 sites along the road where you can stop and learn about the culture and history of the area, or a local landmark. That's if you can tear yourself away from the road!

Start at the corner of US 169 and MN 38. The Blandin Paper mill is on the south side of the street. Turn north on MN 38. You will see signs for the Edge of the Wilderness Scenic Byway.

The road takes you through a residential area of Grand Rapids. Many of the homes were built just after World War II. The homes gradually thin out and the landscape becomes more rural. The two-lane blacktop stretches before you and the speed limit goes up to 55 mph.

The first lake you'll encounter is Prairie Lake. It's big and it stretches alongside the highway for miles. The road curves to fit the terrain. Soon you'll meet a series of hills, dips and curves. The hills come at you fast; Ralph had to downshift to prevent the Victory's engine from lugging. It's a 14-mile rollercoaster ride that rivals the back roads of southern Minnesota's bluff country for beauty and riding challenges.

Hwy. 38 dishes up 14 consecutive miles of hills and curves.

About 21 miles north of Grand Rapids, you'll cross the Laurentian Divide. From this point, water flows northeast toward Hudson's Bay or southeast toward the St. Lawrence Seaway. (If you ride the Gunflint Trail out of Grand Marais, you'll encounter the divide at its northernmost point in Minnesota.)

After you cross Itasca Co. 60, you'll enter the Chippewa National Forest. Evergreens crowd the road, their dark velvet skirts almost brushing the pavement. The air is heavy with their scent.

Lakes such as Bluewater, Grove and North Star flash by. Signs for resorts beckon you off the highway, promising good fishing, good times and sandy beaches. There are more than 100 lakes within a 20-mile radius of the town of Marcell alone.

When you reach Marcell, slow down. The town is named after Andrew Marcell, first conductor of the Minneapolis and Rainy River Railway. (In the latter half of the 19th century, when Minnesota was being settled, the best way to get a place named after you was to work for a railroad or run the local post office.)

Near Marcell, at the intersection of MN 38 and Jack the Horse Resort Road, is the Timberwolf Inn, an unexpected treat in the wilderness. The log-sided inn includes a restaurant, bar and twelve-room hotel and timberwolves feature prominently in the décor. The food is imaginatively flavored and nicely presented. The prices are extremely reasonable. It's easy to see why it's a favorite with local lake home owners and resorters.

As you leave Marcell and head toward Bigfork, the curves are fewer. The Chippewa National Forest disappears, and tamarack swamps take its place. We stopped in Bigfork for gas and groceries. It's a pretty little town, straddling the Big Fork River. Cross the bridge and you're soon on your way to Effie, the last town on MN 38.

It's named after Effie Wenaus, whose mother, Eva, was the village postmaster in 1903. Her father owned the general store that contained the post office. Effie is one of the last places to be settled in the continental United States. There's a bar and a gas station/convenience store, and not much else, although the nearby North Star Ranch does host the <u>North Star Stampede Rodeo</u> the last full weekend in July.

The Edge of the Wilderness byway runs out here, as does MN 38, at the junction with MN 1. MN 1 was completely torn up when we visited, so we turned around and spent the night in Marcell.

Best Hotel

The <u>Timberwolf Inn</u> in Marcell is without a doubt the best hotel we encountered in our travels around Minnesota. Though it has only twelve guest rooms, they are spotless, comfortable and homey. Northwoods décor is the theme, and it's carried out beautifully, with log headboards on the queen beds and quilts chosen individually for each room. Each room looks out over the back of the property, an orchard that will one day serve the restaurant. When we arose, a doe and her fawn made their way across the backyard, stopping to graze here and there amongst the fruit trees.

The Timberwolf also has an excellent restaurant. Real blueberries are in the blueberry pancakes, and the cook knows how to turn an egg "over easy." The steaks are tasty, and the chef specializes in seafood. The cranberry wild rice bread served at the salad bar is a treat. You can also have lunch or drinks on the deck. The Timberwolf is owned and operated by Tim and Brenda Schultz. We highly recommend it!

Minnesota Hwy. 47 North

Minneapolis to Aitkin, 126 miles

With its gentle curves, Minnesota Highway 47 is a pleasant ride that begins in the heart of Northeast Minneapolis and ends "up north." Although you see long lines of traffic on Memorial Day and Independence Day weekends, it's a great alternate to Hwys. 65 and 169 during most summer weekends.

As state highways go, 47 is a young one. In 1940, it was unpaved north of Anoka. The northerly section near Aitkin remained unpaved from 1953-1960. When it was given official state highway designation in 1963, the entire route was paved.

Begin your trip at the corner of University and Central Avenues in Northeast Minneapolis, where University becomes a two-way street. Drive north up the hill past rows of condos and enter a neighborhood of churches, bars and homes dating to the early twentieth century.

The pavement gets rather bumpy as you traverse Lowry Ave. and enter a more industrial area. Say goodbye to Minneapolis as you cross 37th Avenue into Columbia Heights and the speed limit increases to 35 mph. The pavement is smoother when you ride under I-694 and enter Fridley, and the speed increases to 50 mph. Fast food restaurants and service stations are the major employers in this area.

At Foley Blvd. in Coon Rapids, 47 runs together with US 10. Throttle up to 65 mph, and don't be surprised if traffic moves faster. Take the Ferry St. exit in Anoka. The sign will say U.S. 169 South/Hwy. 47 north. Keep to the right and turn onto Ferry St. From here on out, Hwy. 47 becomes a whole lot more interesting.

First is the pair of right-angled turns that sweep you past the Anoka County Fairgrounds. The sheep sheds and cattle barns are empty for most of the cycling season, waiting for their once-a-year glory days in late July. As you leave Anoka, 47 takes on the local name of St. Francis Blvd.

The suburb of Ramsey has seen a lot of growth in recent years, and more is expected as the Northstar Commuter rail line begins stopping there. Almost lost in the crowded jumble of commercial buildings is the quaint, limestone-brick Ramsey town hall, still standing after more than 100 years.

As you exit Ramsey, you'll swoop in and out of a curve over Trott Brook. You'll see more wetlands on either side of the road, and streams that snake between them like black ribbons. As the weather heats up, they emanate an unmistakable, funky fish smell. The town of St. Francis comes into view as you curve around junkyards and apartment buildings on the outskirts of town

Moving northward, you'll encounter the town of Bradford. Although some light industry has begun to move into the area, Bradford looks as though it never quite recovered from the tornado that hit it in the late 1980s-early 1990s. The houses along the highway are scruffy and dingy, in need of paint. Front yards are piled with junk. Pine trees along the east side of 47 still tilt at the angle the wind forced them into years ago. One bright spot is a new eating establishment in the middle of town, <u>Ravens</u>. The restaurant boasts an in-house smoker and wood-fire grill and appears to be a popular stop for bikers.

Continue your journey north, past the Wolcyn Tree Farm on the right, with its rows and rows of evergreens marching across the prairie. You'll cross the Rum River just before you get to the intersection of 47 and MN 95. The intersection is controlled by a semaphore, and there's a gas station/wine and liquor store on the northwest corner of the crossroads.

If you're out riding on a Sunday morning, and it's after 10:00 a.m., stop in for brunch at the Pine Brook Inn on your right. Most items are made from scratch, and the knotty pine paneling creates a comfortable atmosphere. The burgers are a half-pound, and steaks look enormous. It's not uncommon to see a full parking lot there on weekends with quite a few motorcycles among the cars and pickups.

Next up is Dalbo, distinguished by its big fire barn on the south side of town and the creamery. Back in the 1980s, the highway met county roads at right angles, and you headed north to Ogilvie via a one-lane bridge, taking your turn with folks headed south. Today, the angles have been smoothed into curves, and you cross Stanchfield Creek on a two-lane concrete bridge.

It's a straightaway from Dalbo to MN 23. Just before you reach the intersection, you cross the Groundhouse River. Make a left turn at MN 23 and enter Ogilvie. As you make the turn, you'll be confronted with a road that wyes to the right into downtown Ogilvie. If you follow it, it dumps you out on 47 on the west side side of town. Or continue on 23/47 for less than a mile and follow 47 to the right. Cross over the Groundhouse once more, and then you're on your way to Isle.

This old Hwy. 47 landmark may not be around much longer.

Not far from Ogilvie, 47 connects with Kanabec Co. 6. A few miles north, you'll see an abandoned church on the left side of the road. The clapboard siding is weathered gray and the roof has caved in. The arched windows are empty, sightless. The slightest puff of wind would cast the rest of the structure into the tall grass that surrounds it.

As you cruise onward, you'll see Ann Lake on the right. It's a popular fishing hole in the summer, with many boats at the landing. There's a restaurant/nightclub at the top of the hill overlooking the lake. At this writing, it was empty, looking for a new owner.

Hwy. 47 gives you a great ride in this area, alternately climbing hills and diving as the land slowly gains altitude. One of the dives rushes you past a quaint-looking farm on the Knife River. Tamaracks begin to appear in the cattail marshes along the road.

If you travel this area around daybreak or dusk, watch out for deer. They can often be seen grazing in farm fields. Also be on the lookout for patchy fog. Cold air rises from the swamps at night, and wispy fog fingers drift over the highway.

Hwy. 47 gradually cuddles up to Lake Mille Lacs as MN 27 joins it at Isle. As you drive past Terry McQuoid's Resort and cross the Thains River, the highway is surrounded by woods. You can see flashes of Mille Lacs through the trees as you encounter more fishing resorts.

If you need gas or fishing bait, Johnson's Portside Bait & Liquor can supply it. You'll recognize the place instantly: It's flanked by "Massive and Mean" statues of a walleye and a northern pike. The pike may have something in its mouth. Depending on the season, it may be a Halloween pumpkin or a pair of legs.

To get a good view of Mille Lacs, take heed of the brown Scenic Overlook sign on the left side of the highway. Pull off at Vista Road, and take a few minutes to stretch your legs and take a look at the Twin Bays. On a clear day you can look out over the 10,000-acre lake, which the Ojibwe called "Mizi Sagaigon," or "Everywhere" lake. French fur traders translated the word to mean "Thousand Lakes," or "Mille Lacs." On shore there's a geological marker that informs you of the area's geological past.

Mille Lacs creates its own little microclimate, so don't be surprised if the air temperature suddenly feels a lot warmer as you make a left onto 47 and resume your journey. Ice fishing shacks will be parked on either side of the road, waiting for the fall freeze-up. They're a gaudy and colorful mixture of brightly-painted boxes—all the more visible on the ice.

Malmo-and MN 18–is the next crossroads. Named after Malmo, Sweden, it boasts competing gas station/convenience stores and a couple of lively churches.

The highway bends and twists around small lakes and pot-holes as you approach Aitkin. The tiny speck on the map known as Glen pops up at the intersection of 47 and Aitkin Co. 12. If you haven't had lunch, stop in at the Twin Pines Tavern. The burgers are good, and cheap. It's a stop along one of the many snowmobile routes in the area, so the owners and clientele are used to serving travelers as well as locals. In other words, bikers are welcome.

Last the last stretch of 47 coasts you by pine forests, farms and lakes named Dam and Sissabogamauh. It ends abruptly at its junction with US 169 in Aitkin, the seat of Aitkin County and home of its only stoplight. Make a right turn on 169 and drive downtown to the Beanery on Minnesota St. for a good cup of coffee.

Bonus Ride

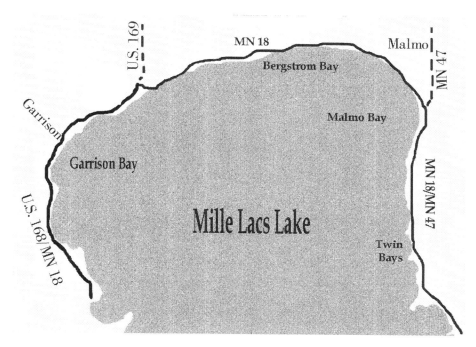

Malmo to Garrison, 21 miles

At the intersection of MN 47 and MN 18 in Malmo, take a left and follow the road as it curves gently around the north shore of Mille Lacs. You'll be rewarded with panoramic views of the lake. It's an especially colorful ride in the fall. MN 18 intersects with US 169, but you can continue to ride MN 18 south around the lake to Garrison.

Capture panoramic views of Lake Mille Lacs on MN 18

Paul Bunyan Scenic National Byway, 54 miles

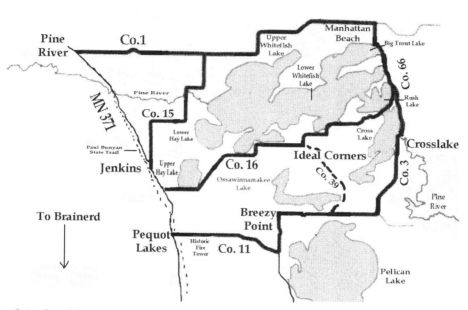

This double-loop drive takes you past sparkling lakes, towering pines and through resort towns along the Whitefish Chain of Lakes. There are fourteen lakes in the Whitefish Chain, which stretches from Pequot Lakes at the southwest end to Manhattan Beach in the northeast.

Quick Directions

US 371 north from Brainerd
Right on Crow Wing Co. 11, 16, 15 or 1
Follow the Byway signs

Take MN 371 north from Brainerd. The divided highway is densely packed with tourist attractions, home furnishings stores and hotels. As you ride, Gull Lake, a popular resort setting, will be on your left. North Long Lake, Round Lake and Lake Hubert will be on your right. You may not notice the difference between the outskirts of Brainerd and the beginnings of Nisswa; the two cities have been growing toward each other for years.

Four lanes narrow down to two as you leave Nisswa. It's a straight shot—and a ten-minute ride—to Pequot Lakes, where the Paul Bunyan Scenic Byway begins.

As you enter Pequot Lakes, don't confuse the Paul Bunyan Trail, a bike and snowmobile trail, with the Paul Bunyan Scenic Byway. Keep a sharp outlook for Crow Wing Co. 11, and take a right through downtown Pequot Lakes. There are many restaurants and little shops in Pequot. Make a mental note and visit one or two at the end of your ride.

The Paul Bunyan byway got its start when Ideal Township petitioned Crow Wing County to pave the shoulders of Co. Rd. 16 to make it safer for bicyclists. (Watch out for them on this route!) Fundraisers were held, and the byway was designated by the State of Minnesota in 1998. Paving was complete in 2002. In 2005, the U.S. Department of Transportation designated the loop as a National Byway for its connection to the mythical lumberjack Paul Bunyan and the family-owned resorts that dot the area. You can download a map from the Paul Bunyan Scenic Byway Association, or pick up a full-size map at an information center.

The byway is all two-lane blacktop and is well marked with images of Paul Bunyan and his trusty companion, Babe the Blue Ox. Information centers are scattered throughout the Byway. You'll recognize them by the signs and by a pair of large, shoe-shaped cement slabs representing Paul's footprints. Many of the signs give Paul's version of historical events.

Paul's footprints lead to interpretive signs

Heading east on Co. 11, you'll see a sign for a historic fire tower on your left. The tower is listed on the National Register of Historic Lookouts. Although you can't climb the tower, there is a trail that leads to a picnic area at its base. You can see the foundation of the cabin that once housed forest rangers and their families.

As you reach the half-way point on Co. 11, the road takes a southerly dip and you find yourself face-to-face with the imposing stone gates of <u>Breezy Point Resort</u>. Breezy has stood on the shores of Pelican Lake for more than eighty years. It was built by Captain Billy Fawcett, creator of "Whiz-Bang" Comics. Gangster

John Dillinger and his crew hid out there during the 1930s, and actors Clark Gable and Carole Lombard vacationed there. Today it's a busy family and convention resort.

Follow 11 as it turns to the left and then makes a hard right. Near the point where the road makes a short little curve, you'll see an osprey nest on the left. It's one of several artificial nesting platforms along the byway.

Take a left at the point where 11 joins Co. Rd. 3 and ride north toward Crosslake. As you enter town, you'll encounter the Crosslake Area Historical Society's Historic Village. The village includes the Ideal Township schoolhouse, built in 1897; the first Crosslake town hall; and several log cabins. It's open 11:00 a.m.-4:00 p.m. weekends Memorial Day through Labor Day.

Just north of Crosslake, you have a decision to make. You can continue north (the road designation changes to Co. 66), or you can angle southward by taking a left onto Co. 16.

A fierce battle between the Dakota and the Ojibwe occurred in this area in 1801. The skinny little neck of land between Cross Lake and Rush Lake was a place where Native Americans camped and collected maple syrup. There's an interpretive sign next to the driveway of the Moonlite Bay restaurant. Stop in and relax on the patio overlooking the lake.

Farther up 66 is the tiny town of Manhattan Beach. Manhattan Beach Lodge is the primary employer. It has stood on the eastern shore of Trout Lake for more than eighty years and is a major wedding destination. The road hugs Trout Lake closely, providing a beautiful view of the water and framed by tall pines.

Co. 66 quickly meets Co. Rd. 1, where you take a left and ride toward the Timothy Town Hall, which was a one-room schoolhouse until it began serving as a civic meeting place.

Cruising along Co. 1, the road curves to the left and then makes a hard right before you come to another decision-making spot at the intersection with Co. Rd. 15. You'll recognize it by the folk art sculpture of two metal horses pulling a wagon. If you continue on Co. 1, you pass a field of boulders, also known as Paul Bunyan's "marbles." Co. 1 meets US 371 at Pine River.

The second option, Co. Rd. 15, travels through some unremarkable farm county before it brings you into Jenkins at US 371. Take 371 south to Co. Rd. 16 and another left just after you see the sign for the Paul Bunyan Roadside Park.

Co. 16 is a much curvier road, and it brings you closer to the lakes. This is the "spine" of the byway. Just a short way up the trail, you'll see a sign for the Veterans Walking Trail. Built to honor World War II veterans, it features a wetlands walkway that takes you to Whiskey Island in Upper Hay Lake. The road skirts Bertha and Clamshell lakes before it leads you into Ideal Corners.

Co. 16 swings close to Pig Lake, named for its porcine shape, as you near the 110-acre Uppgaard Wildlife Management Area. Then it's just a few more gentle curves and you're back at Co. Rd. 66/3.

If you're not quite ready to leave the area and its tall pines and log cabin architecture, take Co. 3 back to Co. 11. Watch for Twp. Rd. 39. Go right on 39, and follow it to Ideal Corners. Although it's not part of the official byway, it's very pretty and you'll run into less traffic, a good thing in the summer. Turn left on Co. 16 at Ideal Corners, and make your way back to US 371.

St. Croix Scenic Byway

Afton to Askov, 125 miles

*Fall is a great time to travel along the St. Croix River. The golds,
bronzes, oranges and reds of autumn make it a spectacular
ride. Spring is just as pretty, with warm winds and the heady*

fragrance of blooming lilacs coming your way. This route takes you north from Afton to Sandstone with plenty of great stops in between. As you travel the "Trail," you'll get a feel for its early importance to Minnesota's lumber industry.

Quick Directions

MN 95 north to US 8, right to Taylors Falls

East on Bench St. to Chisago Co. Rd. 16, go right

At the intersection of Co. Rd. 16 and Hwy. 95 in Amador, turn right

Go right at Co. Rd. 9

Co. 9 becomes Co. 57 in Rush City. Continue north.

Co. 57 becomes MN 361 north of Rush City

Cross west over I-35 at Hinckley to catch MN 61

Connect with MN 23 at Askov

Although Point Douglas near Hastings is the southernmost point of the St. Croix Scenic Byway, we began our ride in Afton, just 15 miles east of St. Paul. The area was first settled in 1837, and its first name was Catfish Bar, after a large sandbar in the St. Croix that still shows up during periods of low water. The name was later changed to Afton, after a Robert Burns poem.

You may want to book a room at the Historic Afton Inn the night before you ride. Built in 1867, it's the oldest operating inn in Minnesota. All 42 rooms are different—one offers a four-poster bed, others offer jacuzzis. For reservations, go to http://www.aftonhouseinn.com. The Afton Inn is also known for its fine dining. Its Current Room offers take-out orders—a good place to pick up a picnic lunch!

MN 95 offers good two-lane blacktop into Bayport. A breeze delivers the fresh-water smell of the St. Croix River as you glide past the Bayport Marina where boats calmly lie at anchor in their protected cove. If you haven't had breakfast yet, stop in at Not Justa Café, 177 3rd Street North. This hole-in-the-wall is known for its hash browns, huge pancakes and a pecan waffle with butterscotch syrup.

If Bayport doesn't appeal to you, continue north into Stillwater. Once a lumberjack town, this stylish riverside city has an abundance of restaurants, antique stores, coffee shops, boutiques and riverboat rides. It's a shopper's paradise and a great place to explore on foot. You could easily end your ride right here!

Although Stillwater is friendly to bikers, it doesn't like noise. Many of Stillwater's historic downtown buildings have been converted to condominiums. As a result, Stillwater has a strict noise ordinance—and the local police enforce it. As you swoop into Stillwater from the south or climb the hills to the north, resist the temptation to rev your engine. The echo's not worth the ticket.

Climbing out of Stillwater on 95, you'll pass limestone bluffs on your left as the St. Croix winds by on the right. The clean scent of pines becomes more prevalent. Pull off at the scenic overlook on the right and take a look back at the city and the boats in the Stillwater marina.

The highway takes you next to Marine-on-St. Croix, site of the first commercial sawmill along the St. Croix. If you're riding on a weekend and feel like trading your bike for somewhat slower transportation, the local riding stable has its horses saddled and ready. History buffs will enjoy the Stonehouse Museum, 241 Fifth Street. Housed in the old city jail, it's open Saturdays and Sundays from Memorial Day to Labor Day.

The next town you'll encounter is Scandia, site of the first Swedish settlement in Minnesota. The Gammelgården Museum, 20880 Olinda Trail, tells the stories of early Swedish settlers via five historic buildings on an 11-acre site. Get there by taking a left off Hwy. 95 at Olinda Trail. Billboards point the way. For hours and programs, check http://www.gammelgardenmuseum.org.

At the intersection of 95 and US 8, turn right and drive to Taylors Falls.

Like Stillwater, the entry into Taylors Falls is a curving, downhill run that takes you right into downtown. Taylors Falls has the distinction of being the site of the world's biggest log jam, back in 1886. Nearly 150 million board feet of logs backed up three miles along the St. Croix from the rapids (where Taylors Falls gets its name). It took 175 men, working around the clock for six weeks, to unclog the mess, which dynamite and towboats couldn't budge. Today, the logjam site is part of Interstate State Park, a collaboration between Minnesota and Wisconsin.

Taylors Falls had another distinguished visitor much earlier in its history. Senator Stephen A. Douglas of Illinois, the "Little Giant" who debated Abraham Lincoln, was a champion of statehood for Minnesota. According to a bronze plaque on the outer wall of the Chisago House Restaurant, he made a speech from the hotel balcony in 1854. (The Chisago House was formerly a hotel, built in 1852. Minnesota Historical Society records show his visit occurred in 1857.)

Regardless of when he showed up, or at all, Stephen Douglas put the Chisago House, 361 Bench Street, on the map. Today it's a good place for an inexpensive breakfast or casual lunch or dinner. You can't miss it—it's right on the corner of Hwy. 95 and Hwy. 8 meet up in Taylors Falls. Just a block east of the Chisago House, you'll find the Drive-In, complete with waitresses in poodle skirts, homemade rootbeer and hand-packed burgers.

The St. Croix Scenic Byway digresses from MN 95 in Taylors Falls. To stay on the byway, drive east on Bench Street about a half mile and take a right at Chisago Co. Rd. 16. You'll pass dairy farms as you wind through the gently rolling hills. Highway signs indicate tractor crossings with a farmer wearing a straw hat and driving a cab-less tractor. Clearly, Chisago County hasn't seen the latest John Deeres.

When Co. Rd. 16 approaches Co. Rd. 12, take a right onto 12, which will bring you to the entrance of Wild River State Park. Wild River offers camping, horseback riding trails and hiking. Get a trail map at the park information station. Find a convenient place to park and take a hike. The River Terrace Loop takes you to a deck that overlooks the former site of the Nevers Dam. While we watched the St. Croix River flow swiftly by, we heard a low rumble that we first mistook for low-flying aircraft. We laughed when we realized it was a group of motorcyclists riding up the Wisconsin side of the river.

Leading away from the park, Co. 16 takes you through Amador where a local artist advertises china painting in the front window of her home. Farther north, 16 runs into Co. Rd. 81, which becomes a dirt road in little less than a mile. It's still part of the St. Croix Scenic Byway. If you'd rather not ride on dirt, backtrack to Amador and Hwy. 95 and take a right. When you reach Co. Rd. 9, take another right. Co. 9 takes you through Sunrise Twp., birthplace of actor Richard Widmark.

Co. 9 winds north through farm country until it hits Rush City, then changes its name to Co. Rd. 57. The blacktop is bumpy and a bit uneven. Co. 57 leaves the north end of town as Minnesota Hwy. 361.

The next stop is Pine City, which takes its name from the Ojibwe word "chengwatana", or pines. If you have the time, we recommend a stop at the North West Company Fur Post, 12551 Voyageur Lane. From Co. 61, take a left on Hillside Ave. N.W. (a.k.a., Co. Rd. 7) and cross I-35. Continue west on Co. 7 (which is named Pokegama Road on the west side of the freeway) until you reach Voyageur Road and take a right.

The North West Company Fur Post takes you back to 1804, and Minnesota's fur-trading days. Run by the Minnesota Historical Society, it gives you a look at how the Ojibwe lived and how their lives changed after European contact. You'll also find out how beaver pelts became the key part of a global economy. For hours and admission costs, visit www.mnhs.org.

Re-cross I-35 to get back to MN 361 and resume your St. Croix Scenic Byway ride. As you cross the Snake River, you'll see, on the left, Pine City's voyageur statue, carved out of redwood and watching over the entrance to the city park. Ride north through Beroun and Mission Creek, then cross the freeway to stop at Hinckley.

Hinckley is known today as the home of the Grand Casino, owned and operated by the Mille Lacs Band of the Ojibwe. In 1894, however, it became famous for the Great Hinckley Fire which swept through the town. In four hours nearly 480 square miles of Minnesota land, towns and farms turned to ash. The Hinckley Fire Museum is located in the old St. Paul & Duluth Railroad Depot on Old Hwy. 61. Check http://www.museum-sofmn.com/hinckley-fire-museum.html for hours and admission

Banning State Park marks a peaceful end to a beautiful ride.

MN 61 parallels I-35 for a little while, then edges west to pass through Friesland. At Sandstone, it connects with MN 23 and takes you to Askov, the end of the line. But don't end your trip there. Stop, instead, in Banning State Park.

Hugging the banks of the Kettle River, Banning State Park was once a thriving quarry. Here, huge sandstone blocks were blasted and cut out of the earth. Many of them were used in construction; smaller blocks were crushed and the resulting chips used in road beds. From 1892 to 1912, sandstone was removed from the area, until the good-quality stone ran out. Now the forest has reclaimed the land. White and red pines scent the air, and the Kettle River rushes past just as it always did. Perch on a rocky ledge and watch kayakers shoot rapids named "Blueberry Slide," "Dragon's Tooth" and "Hell's Gate."

If you visit Banning State Park between May and September, bring plenty of insect spray. The mosquitoes can be relentless, and the forest ranger cautioned us to watch out for ticks.

Worth a Visit

If you've been riding straight through from Afton, the Franconia Sculpture Park is a good place to stop and stretch your legs just before you reach Taylors Falls. The 20-acre park offers work and exhibit space for emerging and established artists from all over the world. It's on the left side of the road, just before the intersection of MN 95 and US 8. Admission is free, although donations are accepted. Wander freely among the sculptures, or have a picnic lunch at one of the tables scattered throughout the park.

Old U.S. 61

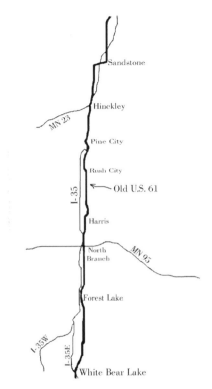

White Bear Lake to Pine City

Driving to Duluth was a lot more fun before I-35 was extended to the port city in the 1980s. Step back in time with a ride along Old U.S. 61.

Quick Directions

Hwy. 61 (White Bear Ave.) N.
Chisago Co. 30 N
MN 361 N
Pine Co. 61 N.
MN 23 runs concurrently with 61

MN 18 runs concurrently with 61 and 23
Carlton Co. 61 N
Carlton Co. 61 N runs concurrently with MN73 and MN27 at
Moose Lake
MN 210 E to Carlton
MN 45 north to Scanlon
Carlton Co. 61 E to the St. Louis Co. line

We picked up US 61 (White Bear Ave.) in White Bear Lake where it meets Ramsey Co. Rd. E. Tousley Ford stands at the northwest corner of the intersection, its old windmill a reminder that this place was "out in the country" back in the 1960s. At one time, US 61 ran 1,400 miles from New Orleans to Canada, but the old road was partially abandoned when the interstate system was built.

Traveling north along White Bear Ave., we passed several car dealerships; Hwy. 61 is the St. Paul suburbs' equivalent of MN 65 in Columbia Heights and Fridley. We left White Bear's quaint downtown and its many stop lights behind us, and White Bear

Lake itself soon appeared on our right, followed shortly by Bald Eagle Lake on our left. Within minutes, we had entered Hugo.

Hugo, once known as the Centerville railroad station, is becoming a manufacturing community. As you enter the south side of town, you'll see that industry is focused on the left side of the highway, while residences line the right. As you exit the north end of the city, industrial sites are on the right and residences are on the left. As you travel along, you get the distinct impression that Hugo is expanding northward, and Forest Lake is stretching southward, and their borders will soon touch.

Hwy. 61 picks up the name of Forest Lake Blvd. as you leave Hugo. It's just eight miles to downtown Forest Lake, where the early morning sun sparkles on the lake. It's fun to curl through the roundabouts and look at the flower baskets overflowing with petunias that adorn the light poles along Lake St. N.

In a little more than four miles, you'll come to the town of Wyoming. As you approach the northern end of town, you'll see signs directing you to I-35 to the west. Ignore them. Stay straight, and you'll see the sign for Old US 61, which runs parallel to the freeway. In fact, you'll never be more than the length of a football field away!

Old 61 changes its name several times as it crosses county lines. In Wyoming it's Chisago Co. 30. At Rush City it becomes MN 361. In Pine County it's Pine Co. 61.

The road from Wyoming though North Branch, Harris, Rush City and Pine City is arrow straight. Ralph forgot to put the bike's kickstand up when we left Harris after a breakfast stop. It stayed down until we had to cross I-35 to follow 61 through Hinckley, and we heard and felt a horrible screech by our left feet. Until that moment, the kickstand had never touched ground.

Hinckley was the scene of a catastrophic fire on September 1, 1894. A grass fire ignited and spread quickly through the area, which had been logged off a couple of years before. The fire covered 400 square miles and killed 418 people. You can find out more about it at the <u>Hinckley Fire Museum</u>, which is open from 10:00 a.m. to 5:00 p.m., Tuesday through Sunday, and on Mondays in July and August. You'll find it on Hwy. 61, just south of Main St.

If the Great Hinckley Fire doesn't interest you, you may find <u>Grand Casino Hinckley</u>, 777 Lady Luck Drive (MN48), more to your liking. Owned and operated by the Mille Lacs Band of the Ojibwe, it's open 24/7/365.

Old 61 winds out of Hinckley and crosses the Grindstone River. At Co. 27 it turns to the right and brings you into Sandstone, home of the Wildcat Sanctuary (not open to the public) and a low-security Federal Correctional Institute for male offenders. If you want to feel a chill, drive down Prison Road toward the window-less building behind the high wire fence.

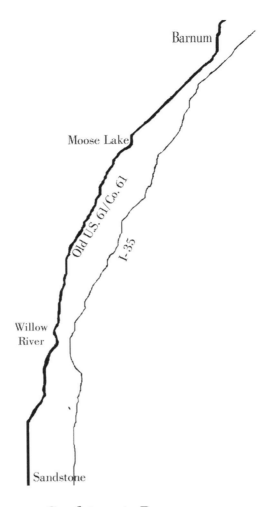

Sandstone to Barnum

Hwy. 61 crosses I-35 to get to Sandstone, then joins MN 123 for a few blocks. The road is renamed MN 23 as you leave town and drive along the western edge of Banning State Park. Soon MN 23 will turn to the right. Stay straight! You are now on MN 18, but underneath it all, it's still Old 61.

The forests begin to show more pines and fewer oaks as you draw near the town of Rutledge, a place that has seen better days. Located on the Kettle River, it once bore that name. Old 61 winds a little, keeping a rough alignment with the river as it flows past the town of Willow River.

Willow River, a pretty little place, is the birthplace of Ernie Nevers, a pro football player who played for the Duluth Eskimos. He was named to the National Football League's 1920s All-Decade Team and elected to the Pro Football Hall of Fame in 1963.

The highway rolls on into Sturgeon Lake where it doubles as Main St., past Sand Lake, the Moose Lake/Carlton County Airport and Coffee Lake before coming to the city of Moose Lake. Just past Mercy Hospital, Hwy. 61 comes to a T with MN 73. Go left to stay on what is now Carlton Co. 61. Within in minutes you'll roll into the town of Barnum. From there, Co. 61 runs in rough parallel with I-35 until it reaches MN 210.

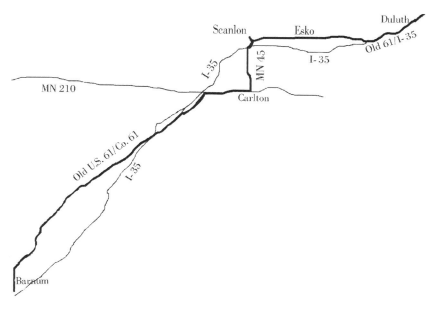

Barnum to Duluth

We rode 210 into Carlton but faced a dilemma. Beyond Carlton, the highway had been completely washed out by torrential rains that had filled Duluth and surrounding areas with water two months before. We rode up to the bridge that crosses the Thomson Resevoir and confirmed the news reports. The road beyond the bridge did not exist. Instead of riding Old 61/MN 210 though Jay Cooke State Park, we had to find an alternate route. We took MN 45 north out of Carlton.

MN 45 was a pleasant, 2.5-mile detour that parallels the St. Louis River. When we reached Scanlon, Old 61 was waiting for us. We turned east toward Esko. As we neared Duluth, we could see the St. Louis River estuary below us, its watery fingers reaching toward Lake Superior. Try as we might, however, we lost the thread of Old 61 and soon found ourselves hurtling past Spirit Mountain and into Duluth via I-35.

Best Breakfast!

We'd been meaning to stop in at the Kaffe Stuga (Swedish for coffee cottage or house) in Harris for a long time. When we did, we were not disappointed. The restaurant is reminiscent of an old Swedish cabin with knotty pine paneling, Dala-style painting and straw goat figurines in the windows. We ordered Swedish apple fritters and ham for breakfast. The first bite of the fritters was an apple-cinnamon explosion in our mouths. The apples were fresh, and the pancake batter was light. The ham—it can only be described as a "slab"—was tasty and flavorful. The Stuga was filled with local customers and bikers who know a good breakfast when they find it. You can't miss it. It's right on Old 61!

North Shore Drive (MN 61)

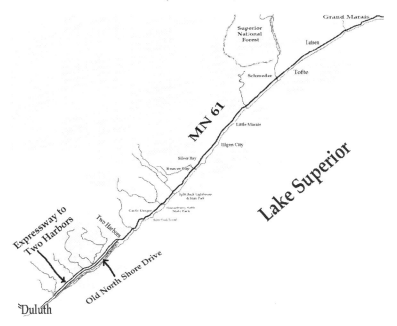

Duluth to Grand Marais, 110 miles

Tell someone you're writing a book about places to ride a motorcycle in Minnesota, and they immediately ask, "Have you done the North Shore?"

With its striking views of Lake Superior, its rugged cliffs and its picturesque towns, the North Shore Drive has long been the poster child for Minnesota tourism. No wonder it was declared an All-American Road—the only road in Minnesota with that designation!

Consider everything the North Shore Drive has to offer: Eight state parks, eight waterfalls, two lighthouses (one is still in operation), Lake Superior, fantastic scenery, plenty of curves, great places to stay and dine, and, if you time it right, not too much traffic.

Scenery draws people to the North Shore with an irresistible magnetic pull, and that can lead to crowding. On summer weekends and weekends during the fall leaf-peeping season, traffic can be bumper-to-bumper from Forest Lake to Grand Marais. Duluth, Two Harbors and Grand Marais can be as crowded with people as the Minnesota State Fair, and hotels, cabins, resorts and condos are booked solid. If you can, travel during the week. There will be room at the inn and traffic will be lessened considerably. Whenever you go, take your time and enjoy the ride.

The North Shore offers something new every season. Spring, after the snow is gone, is the best time to ride the North Shore if you dig waterfalls. Because you're much closer to the North Pole than you would be in Minneapolis, summer days are about 16 hours long, giving you lots of riding time. In the fall, the air is crisp and the leaves are gorgeous.

Begin your ride by taking the Hwy. 61 exit off of I-35. In Duluth, Hwy. 61 is called London Road, and it winds along Lake Superior. Along the way, you'll see the mansions of Duluth's well-to-do. Many of these homes were built in the last part of the 19th Century or early 20th Century. The most famous mansion is Glensheen, built by lumber baron Chester Congdon. Tours of the 7.5-acre estate start every day at 9:30 a.m. You can buy advance tickets online. The tours are very popular, so reserve your tickets early.

As you leave Duluth, you'll cross the Lester River, and Hwy. 61 is briefly renamed Congdon Blvd. Shortly thereafter, you will come to a split. The road to the left takes you to Two Harbors via the expressway. The road to the right is Old Hwy. 61. It's the longer, scenic route. Stay to the right on Congdon Blvd.

The scenic drive from Duluth to Two Harbors takes you past lakefront homes, mom-and-pop resorts and places to buy smoked fish. You'll cross the French River and the Knife River as they empty into Lake Superior. Although you won't always be able to see the lake because of the trees, it is ever-present in the breeze that flows inland.

You'll catch glimpses of beaches and big stretches of wide-open lake. You may see ships—"lakers" that sail the Great Lakes, and "salties" that head out through the St. Lawrence Seaway to the Atlantic Ocean. You can smell the water on the freshening breeze. Watch out for bicyclists on the shoulder along the way. This is a popular bike route. The scenic route meets up with the expressway at Two Harbors.

Two Harbors has catered to tourists for a long time. As you first ride into town, you'll see a giant concrete chicken on the left side of the road. For decades, it's been an invitation to stop at one of the kitchy-est tourist traps you may find.

Two Harbors also boasts many good places to eat and stay and Minnesota's only working lighthouse. The lighthouse flashes its signal three times per minute, all day every day, thanks to volunteers who maintain it. It's a bed-and-breakfast operated by the Lake County Historical Society. Group rates are available. Book early if you want to stay there. If you can't stay, you can tour the lighthouse for $3. Museum hours are Monday - Saturday, 10:00 a.m. - 6:00 p.m. and Sundays from 10:00 a.m. - 4:00 p.m., May through October.

Silver Creek Tunnel

As the road winds along the lakeshore, you'll come to the tunnels at Silver Creek Cliff. Until 1994, when the tunnels were completed, Hwy.61 clung to the side of the cliff. It was a thrilling, hairpin-turn ride. The tunnels have made the ride safer, but less picturesque. The Gitchi Gami bike trail follows the old roadbed around the tunnel on the outside of the cliff. You can still see traces of the old road here and there next to the highway.

Just up the road from the cliffs is Castle Danger. No one is sure how the place got this name, but it's thought that a ship named the Castle ran aground here.

Gooseberry Falls State Park is 13 miles northeast of Two Harbors. With its three sets of waterfalls, Gooseberry is one Minnesota's most visited parks and was the first state park established along the North Shore. It can be quite crowded on summer weekends, but it's worth a visit even if you just stop for a picnic lunch. In dry years you can actually stand in the middle of the riverbed.

After visiting Gooseberry Falls, you'll just get up to cruising speed when you come across <u>Split Rock Lighthouse</u> and State Park. The lighthouse was completed in 1910 and served as a navigational aide until 1969. It's fun to look into Superior's bright blue-green waters from the top of the light. The Minnesota Historical Society (MHS) has restored the light and the light keeper's house. The museum is open seven days a week May 15 through October 15, from 10:00 a.m. to 6:00 p.m. Admission is $9 for adults; MHS members get in free.

After Split Rock it's on to Beaver Bay, Silver Bay and Illgen City, towns that owe their livelihood to the iron-mining industry as much as they do to tourism. (Silver Bay was established in 1952 when Reserve Mining platted the town.) You can watch ore ships take on a load of taconite at Silver Bay. Or look down to Lake Superior from the top of Palisade Head, part of <u>Tettegouche State Park</u> where the Baptism River takes a 60-ft. dive into Lake Superior.

Sections of blacktop in this area were so fresh, we could smell the tar.

Coniferous forests begin to dominate the landscape. Oaks and maples give way to birches, aspen and pine. As you continue northward, cedar begins to blend in, adding a new spice to the fresh breezes coming off the lake. The two-lane highway is in good condition. Occasional pull-outs for sight-seeing and bypass lanes for slower traffic make the ride more enjoyable.

From Beaver Bay to Grand Marais, the highway sticks close to the shore, as if reluctant to let the lake out of its sight. You'll encounter all kinds of hotels, motels, lodges, mom-and-pop cabin resorts and luxury resorts such as Lutsen and Blue Fin

Bay. And more state parks, including Temperance River and Cascade River. Stop at the Cascade pullout and take time to watch the Cascade's coffee-colored waters tumble and swirl into Lake Superior.

You enter Grand Marais with a downhill swoosh that brings you smartly down to the waterfront. Seagulls hover over the breakwater and look for fish or French fries; they're not fussy. The Coast Guard's automated light stands out in the harbor as it has since the 1920s.

Grand Marais' eclectic downtown is opposite the harbor. Once a logging community, the town is a major jumping-off point for paddlers setting off into the Boundary Waters Canoe Area Wilderness (BWCAW). There are still outfitters in town and along the Gunflint Trail to send them on their way. More recently, the town has become an art colony, and the retail "mix" reflects that change, although you can still get a heavy-duty Woolrich shirt at Joynes' Department Store. Restaurants are plentiful; menus vary from Tex-Mex to gourmet French. There's a fudge shop, of course. For a good, cheap sandwich or pizza, Sven and Ole's, 9 Wisconsin Ave., is the place to be. If you're looking for a place that serves a good selection of micro-brews, head to the Gunflint Tavern, just south of Sven and Ole's at 111 W. Wisconsin.

After kicking back in Grand Marais, you'll want to get back on the highway. The pavement on MN 61 north of Grand Marais is rougher than the road to the south. It's less traveled, but it's the main lifeline for Minnesotans who live along it.

Croftville is just three miles up the road—you'll breeze right through it. On your right, you'll see the looming hulk of Five Mile Rock. It was used as a navigational aid for hundreds of years and is five miles from Grand Marais.

Grand Marais to Grand Portage, 30 miles

Fourteen miles northeast of Grand Marais, the stately Naniboujou Lodge dominates the shoreline. Built as a private club in the 1920s, it's on the National Register of Historic Places. The lodge dining room is known for its Cree Indian decorative motif. There are no TVs or Wi-Fi, and cell service is limited. It's open full time from mid-May to mid-October, and weekends after that.

On your way to Hovland, you'll cross the Kadunce and Brule Rivers and come to the borders of Judge C.B. Magney State Park. Magney established eleven North Shore state parks and waysides during his tenure as judge, so it's appropriate that one was named for him.

Just past Hovland, you'll enter the Grand Portage Indian Reservation. This area was one of the first Ojibwe settlements in Minnesota, and the community today has more than 500 members, half of whom are enrolled in the Grand Portage Band of Lake Superior Chippewa. The band runs the Grand Portage Lodge and Casino which offers gambling on a 24-hour basis.

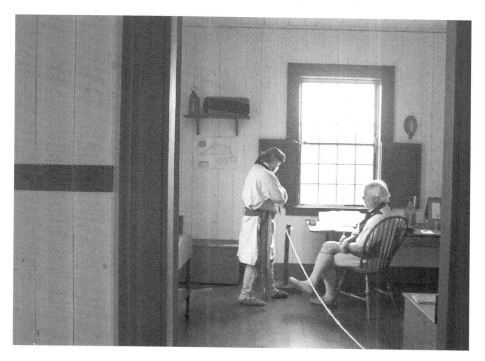

Re-enactors at Grand Portage National Monument

Grand Portage was the center of the fur trade in Minnesota. Voyageurs roamed the rivers and lakes in the area and brought furs and pelts down the Pigeon River to Lake Superior. The last nine miles of the river had to be circumnavigated because of a number of waterfalls that make canoeing nearly impossible. "Grand portage" is the French translation of "big carrying place." Men carried their 90-lb. packs of furs and their canoes down to the Lake Superior shore along this heavily wooded trail. A stockade was built there in the 1600s and a lively trading post grew up at the edge of the lake. In the 1950s Grand

Portage was proclaimed a national monument, and the stockade and some of the post buildings were rebuilt. A Heritage Center was added in 2007.

The biggest event of the year at Grand Portage is Rendezvous Days and Powwow, held in mid-August. Fur trade re-enactors and Native Americans gather to celebrate the time in summer when the French voyageurs came out of the woods to deliver their goods to traders on the shore. There are lacrosse games, 18th-century foods and music and craft demonstrations. The re-enactors camp at Grand Portage National Monument; the powwow takes place on the reservation. All are welcome to participate, and it's a busy, crowded place. It's nearly impossible to find a hotel room or campsite between Duluth and Grand Portage during Rendezvous Days.

It's just a little more than six miles from the monument to the Canadian border. If you're heading into Canada, make sure you have your U. S. passport ready. Border security is tighter than it used to be, and you'll need it for re-entry into the States.

If you're not going on, you can turn around and have the pleasure of riding MN 61—southbound.

Gunflint Trail National Scenic Byway (Cook Co. 12)

Grand Marais to Seagull Lake, 57 miles

It seemed almost sacrilegious to ride a motorcycle up the Gunflint. It is, after all, the eastern entrance to the Boundary Waters Canoe Area Wilderness (BWCAW, where motorized traffic of any kind is outlawed. It also happens to be one of the best bike rides in Minnesota.

It had been a while since we'd traveled up the Gunflint, and more than 30 years since we had first paddled and portaged our way through the BWCA. Things were bound to be different. But we didn't expect Cook County to move the trailhead!

The old "entrance" to the Gunflint was (and still is) marked by the figures of a voyageur portaging a canoe and a bear riding a boat. It's late '50s, early '60s kitsch, and it has marked the beginnings of many a canoe voyage. You'll find the voyageur and his friend on the corner of First St. and 2nd Ave. W., next to the Grand Marais Public Library.

The new entrance is on the north side of town at the intersection of MN 61 and Cook Co. 12. Take a left. A big new sign welcomes you to the Gunflint Trail. The two-lane road is newly paved, black and smooth. It winds in a northwesterly direction out the "back" of Grand Marais and into the wilderness. A water tower emblazoned with a moose beckons you onward.

The Gunflint is an old trail used for centuries by Indians and later by voyageurs and fur traders who visited the area. It gets its name from the flint the Europeans found along the lakeshores; they used it to strike a spark on the little pan of gunpowder on their rifles, which caused a bullet to fly out the bore on the other end. Prospectors showed up in the mid-1800s, looking for minerals, and the trail became a road. Loggers came in the 1880s. The area began its shift toward recreation in the 1920s. Many of the lodges along the trail have been in operation since the 1940s. The Gunflint was designated a National Scenic Byway in 2009.

As we left Grand Marais, Lake Superior receded in the distance, and we were soon surrounded by tall pines, aspen and birch. The air had a fresh, spicy scent.

About two and a half miles out of town, we came to Cook Co. 53, also known as Pincushion Drive. If you take a right, there is a lookout about a quarter of a mile down the road where you can look out over Grand Marais and Lake Superior.

The Devil Track River is two miles further up the trail, followed by the Gunflint Hills Golf Course on the right. At six miles up the trail, we were greeted with the smell of fresh-sawn lumber.

Family-owned Hedstrom Lumber Company has been operating on the Gunflint since 1914.

The Gunflint offers numerous satisfying curves.

Not far from Hedstrom's are the George Washington Memorial Pines, planted in 1932 by Grand Marais Boy Scouts in commemoration of the first president's birthday. A few miles beyond are the famous Gunflint Pines, a stand of old-growth Eastern white pines estimated to be 350 years old.

As we rode further, the wilderness took over. Forest roads lead to the left or right; they are not paved. We saw occasional signs for lodges and campgrounds, but they're off the trail, deeper into the woods. We found ourselves on the lookout for deer on the edges of the woods and moose in the swampy areas.

The road snaked through the Superior National Forest, around swamps, over hills. Bright-pink fireweed lined the roadsides, a lovely contrast to the deep dark pines. The Trail curved around lakes, always drawing us farther north and west. There is an ancient quality to the land.

When we crossed the South Brule River, the land suddenly looked empty. This is where a derecho wind swept through in 1999, knocking down more than 477,000 acres of timber. Young birches and aspen are beginning to take the place of the towering pines that stood here. As we approached Hungry Jack Lake, a sign on the right told us about the wildfire that swept through here in 1967. We began to realize just how little control humans have over this country.

Poplar Lake is the approximate mid-point of the Gunflint Trail. There are some shops here, and you can get a good lunch and some souvenirs at Trail Center. But the road has its own siren call, so you keep riding.

The road rises, and we found ourselves at the top of a hill. A U.S. Forest Service sign announced that we'd reached the Laurentian Divide Scenic Overlook. It's from this point that water flows north into Hudson Bay or east into the St. Lawrence watershed. The overlook is quite overgrown, but there are stairs leading down to Birch Lake.

On the downhill side of the divide are swampy areas where moose like to graze. The pavement got rougher as we rode past Loon Lake Road (Co. 51). The land looks more barren, too. Granite outcroppings that were once covered by pine forests poke up from the landscape. Skeletal trees stand in silence, perhaps a few sprigs of green topping their burnt bodies.

The forest began to reappear as we approached the end of the road. A phone booth stands at the end of the trail. The pages of the phone books are torn and yellowed with age, but it's the only phone that works out here. Cellular service is non-existent. Beyond the phone booth are Seagull Lake and the Boundary Waters.

We stopped in at Way of the Wilderness' Trail's End Café for a burger and talked motorcycling with some bikers on their way home to Fargo. After lunch we gazed for a while at Seagull Lake and prepared to retrace our route along the Gunflint.

It's the only way back to Grand Marais.

Cell phones don't work at the end of the Gunflint Trail.

Worth a Stop

Chik-Wauk Museum and Nature Center

As you near the end of the Gunflint, you'll see a turn for Co. Rd. 81 (Moose Pond Drive). Take the turn and drive one-quarter of a mile down a gravel road to the <u>Chik-Wauk Museum and Nature Center</u>. Once a family-owned lodge, it's now a 50-acre nature preserve along the shore of Saganaga Lake. It's run by volunteers of the Gunflint Trail Historical Society in cooperation with the U.S. Forest Service (which is why you see Property of U.S. Government signs all over the place.)

The old stone lodge, built during the Great Depression, serves as an interpretive center where you can view exhibits about the people who carved a living out of the wilderness, from Native Americans to the pioneering "resorters" of the 1930s and '40s. Naturalists give talks, and there are several trails to hike. Admission is $3 per adult. Chik-Wauk (thought to be the Ojibwe word for white pine) is open May-October.

Veterans Evergreen Memorial Highway, MN 23

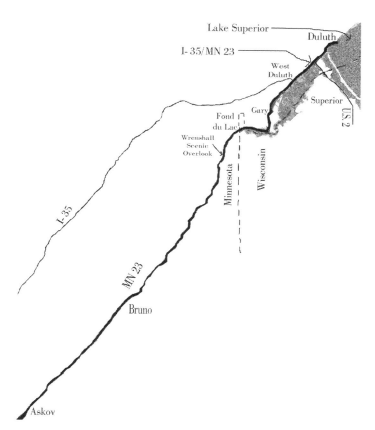

Duluth to Askov, 58 miles

Quick Directions

Grand Ave. exit, I-35, Duluth
South on MN 23 (Grand Ave.-Commonwealth Ave.)

Tree-lined and curvy, this section of MN 23 is a biker's delight.

83

This road has been known for decades as the scenic road to Duluth. Fortunately, the scenery is just as nice leading *from* Duluth!

Pick up MN 23 at the Grand Ave. exit off I-35 in downtown Duluth. The avenue brings you through a tired-looking area of Duluth, past Indian Point Park and the Lake Superior Zoo. Continue south through the Smithville neighborhood into Gary, where Grand Ave. becomes Commonwealth Ave. Gary soon runs into the St. Louis River, and MN 23 curves to the right toward Fond du Lac.

As you leave Fond du Lac, MN 23 divides. The right fork becomes MN 210 and goes through Jay Cooke State Park. The left fork crosses the St. Louis River and continues southward as MN 23. Black Bear Casino, owned and operated by the Fond du Lac Ojibwe, is nearby. You can't miss its flashing lights.

The bridge across the St. Louis is the Biauswah Bridge, named after an Ojibwe chief, Biauswah, who gave his life for his son, also named Biauswah. The bridge honors Native American veterans.

Just after you cross the bridge, you'll drive through a tiny sliver of Wisconsin. There are no signs to tell you this, and your re-entry into Minnesota will go unnoticed. Continue south until you get to the Wrenshall Scenic Overlook. Pull over and take a pause. From the concrete wall you can see Jay Cooke State Park and the St. Louis River.

The Wrenshall Overlook

The overlook is what remains of a bigger scenic overlook built in the late 1940s. It was dedicated to World War I veterans from Carlton, Pine and St. Louis counties. One of the plaques on the overlook wall is for them. Another is dedicated to Vietnam veterans, and the other commemorates the efforts of people who fought in World War II. The overlook was rededicated in 1991.

Beyond the overlook, the drive down MN 23 curves gently along forests and occasional farm fields. Evergreens line the roadsides like the soldiers they honor. On the way are little towns that almost don't exist anymore—Nickerson, Duquette, Kerrick, and Bruno.

We stopped at the Bear's Den Tavern in Bruno for lunch. The food won't win any gourmet awards, and the beer selection is limited, but the owners ride motorcycles, and they give bikers a warm welcome. Like a box of Crackerjack candy, the Bear's Den has a surprise inside. It comes in the form of a black bear that met its demise on the highway. Mounted inside a glass case, "Bruno" has found a good home at the Bear's Den.

It's just a little more than eight miles from Bruno to Askov with a ride through the DAR Memorial State Forest. The land was donated to the state by the Daughters of the American Revolution in 1929.

Askov proclaims itself the "Rutabaga Capital of the World" and celebrates this lowly vegetable every August. The area was settled by Danes in the early 1900s, and the town's name means "ash forest" in Danish. MN 23 curls like a ribbon through town before heading southwest to Sandstone and I-35. The evergreens have thinned out. You're back on the Minnesota prairie once again.

The Southwest

Hints of the American West

Just before it achieved statehood, Minnesota was part of the American West, and the southwest corner of the state was the gateway. It's the area where the U.S.-Dakota War of 1862 started, and where the Indians began a long defense of their homelands that spread into Montana (Battle of the Little Bighorn, 1876) and ended in South Dakota (Wounded Knee, 1890). It's history and riding rolled up into one great package.

Minnesota River Scenic Byway

Although the Minnesota River Scenic Byway begins in Browns Valley, on Minnesota's western edge, we connected with the route on U.S. 75 in Ortonville. If you'd like turn-by-turn directions going east to west, visit <u>America's Byways</u>. (Of course, you can also follow the directions in reverse order.) You can also get a map from <u>www.mnrivervalley.com</u>.

Caution: There are gaps in the byway, and the trail is not well marked. Segments of this byway are gravel road.

Quick Directions

U.S. 75 east from Ortonville
Lac Qui Parle Co. 38 to Co. Rd. 34
Turn right (south) on MN 119 to Lac Qui Parle Co. 20
20 becomes Chippewa Co. 14
Take 14 to U.S. 59/MN 7 to Montevideo
Co. 15 to Co. 5 to Granite Falls
OR take U.S. 212 to Granite Falls
MN 67 to Co. 81 to Co. 15 to Morton
MN 19 to Co. 5 to Co. 21 to MN 15 to New Ulm
MN 68 to Mankato
Riverfront Drive to Third
Third becomes Blue Earth Co. 5, then LeSueur Co. 21
LeSueur Co. 21 to MN 22
MN 22 to MN 99 to LeSueur Co. 23 to Ottawa
LeSueur Co. 36 from Ottawa to MN 93/U.S. 169
Take 93 left to Henderson
Sibley Co. 6 from Henderson to Belle Plaine

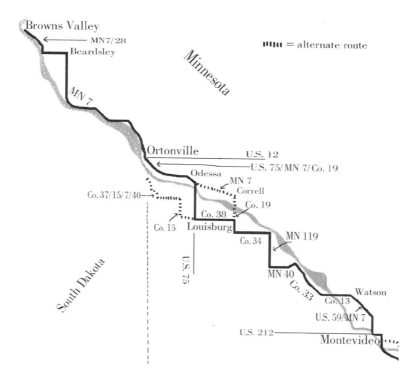

Browns Valley to Montevideo

This route follows the Minnesota River. Along the way, you'll encounter many historic sites connected with the U.S.-Dakota Conflict of 1862. There are several gaps in the route, and markings aren't always clear. It's a confusing mélange of paved and gravel roads and Alternate Byway paved and gravel roads. You have to be eagle-eyed to spot the byway designation, a bald eagle on a fuschia background.

From Ortonville, head south on US 75. You'll pass through Odessa, a little town that's been steadily shrinking in area and population for more than a decade. Continue traveling south on 75 until you reach Lac Qui Parle Co. Rd. 38. Turn left (east), and drive into Louisburg, a tiny town of 47 people. Remnants of a gas station and a 1911 school are the most prominent land-marks here. Follow 38 until you reach Co. Rd. 34. Go east, young man!

When you encounter MN 119, turn right. You're near the Lac Qui Parle Wildlife Area. "Lac Qui Parle" is a French translation for the Dakota word that means "lake that speaks." Lac Qui Parle Lake is a spring and fall pit stop for migrating geese. The birds' honking racket can be heard for a long distance.

Take 119 south past its junction with MN 40 to Lac Qui Parle Co. Rd. 20. Lac Qui Parle State Park lies along 20. You'll find the road alternates several times between stretches of blacktop and gravel. Take your time—the changes from one surface to another are abrupt.

As it crosses into Chippewa County, Co. 20 becomes Co. 14. It's a short distance to US 59/MN 7, which will bring you into Montevideo. If you're ready for lunch and you like Chinese food, the Grand Buffet at 207 N. First St. offers a surprisingly good buffet. The staff is clearly learning English, but you'll find potstickers and fried rice and other Asian foods on the steam tables. And a curiously Minnesotan addition—tater tots.

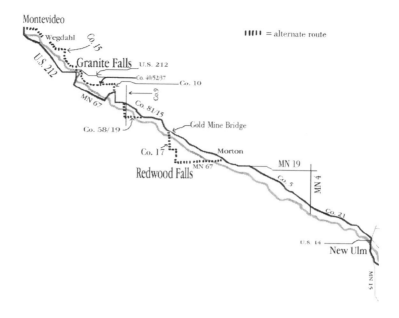

Montevideo to New Ulm

The byway becomes confusing as you leave Montevideo and begin to encounter gravel and gaps! The gaps occur because you'll pass through commercial and industrial areas and other places deemed "non-scenic." Signs point you to alternate routes that may or may not be paved.

We took US 212 southeast out of Montevideo. We saw a byway sign pointing toward Chippewa Co. 15, turned left onto it and ran into alternating stretches of paved road and gravel. The road follows the Minnesota as it squirms through the countryside. The humidity-filled air did nothing to dampen the dust that plumed behind us and settled on the leaves of the corn and soybeans that filled the river bottoms.

Co. 15 makes a couple of right-angle drops until it reaches Co. Rd. 5 (30th Ave. S.). We turned right onto 5 and followed it into Granite Falls.

We skirted the east side of Granite Falls on 30th, which connected us first with Oak Street and then John Other Day Road. (John Other Day was a Dakota who helped white settlers in New Ulm during the Dakota War. For this, he was rewarded by Congress and reviled by his fellow Dakota.) John Other Day Road crosses 212 and connects with Pete's Point Road (Renville Co. 40). We traveled along Pete's Point, crossing Renville Co. 37.

As it reaches Co. 37, Co. Rd. 40 is designated 810th Ave. We followed 810th to Co. Rd. 10 and turned south, which brought us back to Co. Rd. 15, now called Renville Co. 15.

Along the way we encountered the Joseph R. Brown Wayside Memorial. Brown was, among many things, an Indian agent, and was married to a Dakota woman. There's a picnic table here, sited among the ruins of Brown's house which was burned by the Indians during the war.

Further down the road, where 15 and Co. Rd. 1 meet and run together for a few feet, you'll find the unlikely site of a grave marker, standing almost literally in a farmer's driveway. It's the Schwandt State Memorial, placed there in 1915 to commemorate the killing of Johann and Christina Schwandt and their family during the Dakota conflict.

The corn and soybean fields, flanked by woods along the Minnesota River, were a lush emerald green. They would have been restful to look at if we didn't have to spend every second being aware of the pavement (or lack of it) beneath our wheels.

We continued along 15, riding carefully along the gravel parts and speeding up when we hit blacktop until we came to the junction of 15 and Co. Rd. 21. There, the lack of signs threw us for a loop, and we crossed south over the river on 21.

One of the joys of taking wrong turns is that you discover something truly unexpected. In this case, it's a through truss bridge with a wooden deck that's eligible for National Register of Historic Places status. Although it's rated as "structurally deficient," 475 vehicles still cross it every day. It's known as the Gold Mine Bridge. The highway signs change from Co. 21 to Co. 17 as you cross the bridge into Redwood County. We later found out that this "wrong turn" is one of the "alternate" byway routes.

The Gold Mine Bridge

We passed through North Redwood, the town where Richard Warren Sears started the mail order business that became Sears Roebuck and Co. When we found ourselves in Redwood Falls, we turned left onto Hwy. 19 and headed, gratefully, on two-lane blacktop to Fairfax, skipping over a 20-mile course of meandering gravel.

To get back to the byway, we traveled south on Minnesota Hwy. 4.

If you want to stick to the byway, take 19 east out of Morton until you reach Nicollet Co. Rd. 5, which angles to the southeast.

About halfway to New Ulm, Co. 5 becomes Co. 21. It's a smooth ride on 21 which connects with MN 15 to bring you into New Ulm.

If you've never visited New Ulm, try to allow a day or two. This very German city is home to <u>August Schell Brewing</u>, founded in 1860, and still family-owned. Tours run daily Memorial Day through Labor Day and on a more limited schedule throughout the rest of the year. Check the website for hours.

New Ulm also has great shopping, especially along Minnesota Street. The <u>Brown County Historical Society Museum</u>, 2 N. Broadway, gives you all the details about the Battle of New Ulm. The Minnesota Music Hall of Fame is headquartered here. Don't forget to visit the statue of Hermann the German. You can climb to the top of his observation tower for a small fee and get a great view of the Minnesota River Valley. If you're looking for German food, head to <u>Veigel's Kaiserhoff</u> at 221 Minnesota. You can get a great farm-style breakfast at <u>Joni's Restaurant & Catering</u> at 24 N. Minnesota.

New Ulm to Belle Plaine

To continue on, take MN 15 south out of New Ulm. When you cross the river, it becomes MN 68. You'll wind through Cambria, and Judson. Just before you reach Mankato, you'll see signs for <u>Minneopa State Park</u>. *Minneopa* is a Dakota word meaning, "water falling twice." The double waterfalls in this park are worth making a stop. The Seppmann Mill, a wind-driven grist mill built in the German style with stone and wood, is also in the park.

Minneopa Falls near Mankato

Continue on 68 into Mankato. Here again, the byway signs are hard to detect. The byway map routes you through downtown

Mankato, along Riverfront Drive, past Reconciliation Park. Here a statue of a white buffalo marks the spot where 38 Dakota were hanged in 1862. It was the only mass execution ever to take place on U.S. soil.

Riverfront Drive connects with Third Ave. Take a left onto Third which will become Blue Earth Co. 5. Travel on to the town of Kasota. Co. 5 becomes LeSueur Co. 21 at Kasota and will soon bring you to MN 22. Take 22 north into St. Peter and US 169. In St. Peter, take a quick jog from 169 onto MN 99 (Broadway Ave.), then make a quick angle to the left onto LeSueur Co. 23. Also known as the Ottawa Road, it will take you through the Ottawa State Wildlife Management Area, past the Ottawa Bluffs and into the town of Ottawa.

At 390th St., take a left to rejoin the Ottawa Road (now called Co. Rd. 36). This will lead you into LeSueur, and the home of Dr. W.W. Mayo, founder of the Mayo Clinic. Stop for a visit if you have time. If not, cruise past the house, cross the river and get onto US 169/MN 93.

Because we missed the signs, we ended up taking US 169 north out of Mankato, through St. Peter to the 169/MN 93 split.

When 93 splits from 169, follow it left into the quaint little town of Henderson. Continue through Henderson, but watch for the sign for Sibley Co. 6 to take you into Belle Plaine, the end of your journey.

Worth a Stop

A stop at Ft. Ridgely State Park, seven miles south on the corner of Hwy. 4 and Nicollet Co. Rd. 30, is a great chance to stretch your legs. Take a right and drive up Co. 30. When you get to the fork, stay right and enter the park.

Ft. Ridgely was an active fort during the Dakota conflict. You can wander through the ruins, take in a video at the museum, hike, golf, fish or camp. The park is open Memorial Day weekend to Labor Day, 8:00 a.m.-8:00 p.m. <u>Museum</u> admission is $4 for adults.

Just across the road from the Co. 4/Co. 30 confluence is Co. Rd. 21. Make a slight jog and drive southeast toward New Ulm. Before you get there, however, you'll see the <u>Harkin Store</u> tucked up in the trees opposite the river bank. On the other side of the road is the steamboat landing where supplies for the area's pioneer families were brought. When the railroad came to New Ulm, the store was abandoned. The merchandise remained on its shelves. It's now managed by the Nicollet County Historical Society for the Minnesota Historical Society. It's open Tuesday through Sunday, Memorial Day weekend through Labor Day, and on weekends in May, September and October. The parking area at the Harkin Store is tiny; choose your spot carefully so your bike doesn't roll down into the river.

The Harkin Store

Minneapolis-Pipestone, 200 miles

Quick Directions

US 212 west to Granite Falls
MN 23 south to Pipestone
US 75 south to Luverne

This ride is a straightforward diagonal run down to the southwestern corner of Minnesota, but it has its own scenic and riding pleasures.

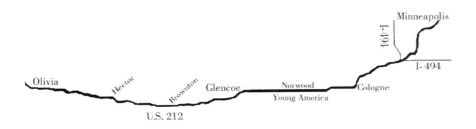

Minneapolis to Olivia

Catch US 212 heading west out of Minneapolis. As you leave Edina and Eden Prairie behind, you'll encounter gently rolling hills and curves on this four-lane concrete highway. You'll enter farm country as you roll past Shakopee and Chaska. Fields of corn and soybeans line the highway, and you'll see signs for fresh eggs, sweet corn or apples, depending on the season.

Just west of Cologne is the hamlet of Bongards. Make plans to stop in at the Bongards' Creamery retail store at the intersection of 212 and Carver Co. 51. This farmer cooperative, started in 1908, offers a large selection of cheeses made in the creamery next door. You can pick up blocks or loaves of cheese—or maybe just grab some fresh cheese curds for a snack. They also have T-shirts and hoodies in case you need a little extra clothing under your leathers. The store is open 6:30 a.m.-7:00 p.m. weekdays and 9:00 a.m-5:00 p.m. Saturdays and Sundays.

If you bypassed the creamery but haven't had breakfast yet, stop in at <u>Bump's Family Restaurant</u> in at the stoplight in Glencoe. On the left side of the intersection, it's a gathering spot for farmers and workers in the area, and it offers home cooking at a reasonable price.

Hwy. 212 shrinks to two lanes as you head west from Glencoe. As you come upon each town along the way, your brain soon recalls a recitation of winter school closings on WCCO-Radio: Buffalo Lake, Hector, Bird Island, Olivia, Danube, Renville, Sacred Heart. To reinforce the idea that you really are in an area where agriculture is the biggest business in town, each city has an implement dealer on its outskirts and a grain elevator in the center.

On a hill just east of Renville is the Birch Coulee Memorial which commemorates the battle fought nearby by settlers and the Dakota Indians. The memorial—two granite monuments shaped like arrows— honors the settlers who fought and the "good" Indians who helped them. It's at the end of a steep gravel driveway that gives you a slow, nail-biting ride on the way up and on the return trip down. Go there only if you're experienced in riding on gravel. It doesn't take much for the rear wheels of your bike to slide sideways.

The town of Renville houses the Renville County Museum. For $2, you can see the preserved artifacts of the area's pioneer families or do some genealogical research.

Back on 212, the road becomes a four-lane highway again as you near Granite Falls.

The Minnesota River Valley near Granite Falls

Pull over at the scenic overlook on the left side of the highway just before you enter Granite Falls. Take a look at the Minnesota River valley stretching below you. A bronze marker placed at the overlook by the Minnesota Department of Transportation explains how the valley was formed and tells you that ancient bison-butchering sites have been found across the river.

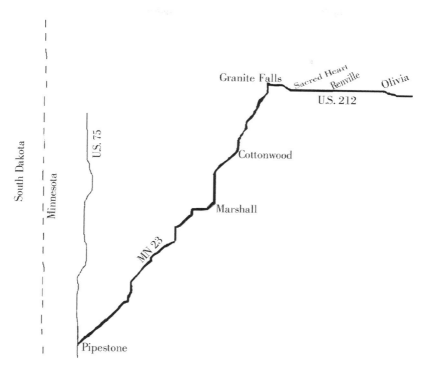

Olivia to Pipestone

It's less than a mile from the overlook to the intersection of 212 and MN 23. Cross the bridge into Yellow Medicine County, turn left at the light and go south toward Marshall.

Hanley Falls is one of the towns along the way as you angle toward the southwest corner of the state. The Minnesota Machinery Museum will be on your left. If you have time, stop in and see how the old Hanley Falls School has been transformed into an agricultural learning center. Five buildings on the grounds house restored farm equipment, some of it dating back to the early 1900s. The museum is open from May through September. Museum hours are from 10:00 a.m. to 4:00 p.m. Monday through Saturday; Sunday 1:00 to 4:30 p.m. For more information, visit www.mnmachinerymuseum.com.

Continue down 23 through Marshall, the home of Southwest Minnesota State University and the Schwans Food Company. MN 23 runs in four lanes from Marshall to Lynd when it resumes its two-lane format once again.

It's a 40-minute ride from Marshall to Pipestone, a good place to stop for the night. You'll notice some subtle changes in scenery. Outcroppings of pink Sioux quartzite will appear. Corn and bean fields will be replaced here and there by herds of Angus or Hereford cattle. There's a hint of the Old West in the landscape.

As you near Pipestone, the Buffalo Ridge wind farms stretch as far as you can see any in any direction. This is one of the windiest places in Minnesota, and upwards of 600 wind turbines dot the 60-mile-long-ridge which runs through Lincoln, Pipestone, Murray and Nobles Counties. Their graceful arms spin majestically in the clear prairie air.

MN 23 intersects and runs with US 75 in Pipestone. Drive two blocks, take a left from 75/23 onto Main Street, then go right. You are now in the heart of historic Pipestone and at the door of the Historic Calumet Inn.

The Calumet opened for business on Thanksgiving Day in 1888. Built of Sioux quartzite mined at nearby Jasper, it's on the National Register of Historic Places. It was renovated in the late 1970s. The bank vault on the first floor is now a lounge. The rooms are comfortable, and the restaurant serves great steaks for about half the price of a steak in Minneapolis. It's biker friendly. Check www.calumetinn.com for more information or to make reservations.

The other main drag in Pipestone is Hiawatha Avenue, and it takes you to the Pipestone National Monument. This is where Native Americans from all over the U.S. come to quarry the sacred red rock known as catlinite, or pipestone. This is the only place in the world where this stone is found, and they are the only people allowed to quarry there. President Franklin Roosevelt and Congress declared it a national monument in 1937.

Old Stone Face, Pipestone National Monument

When you visit, be sure to take in the 22-minute movie that explains the pipestone's significance to Native Americans. Depending on when you visit, you can see artisans working the soft, dark-red stone, shaping it into jewelry, figurines and pipes. After the movie, head outdoors and hike the ¾-mile Circle Trail. It's an easy, circular walk that takes you to Winnewissa Falls and rock formations such as the Old Man and the Oracle, as well as the actual quarries. You will probably come across Native American prayer flags and gifts of sage at various points along the trail. Leave them alone: you're on hallowed ground. The monument is open year-round, 8:00 a.m. to 5:00 p.m. every day except Thanksgiving, Christmas and New Year's. Admission is $3 and is good for seven days.

After hiking the monument, you'll have worked up an appetite. Head over to Lange's at 110 8th Ave. S.E. Lange's is famous for pies. Its sour cream raisin pie was praised by National Public Radio food critics Michael and Jane Stern as the "best sour cream raisin pie ever made." Open 24/7, it dishes out a mean hot roast beef sandwich (also known as a "commercial"), complete with real mashed potatoes and gravy.

There are other interesting places to visit in Pipestone—the Keepers of the Sacred Tradition of Pipemakers where you can learn more about pipe-making, Ft. Pipestone, and the Pipestone County Museum, just across the street from the Calumet Inn.

Worth the Visit

If you like history, take a detour at Olivia on US 71, heading south to Morton on MN 19. On 19, head east to Redwood Co. 2, then south on 2 to the Lower Sioux Agency.

Lower Sioux is where Minnesota's "other Civil War" began. In 1853, the Dakota people made a treaty with the U.S. government at Traverse des Sioux (near St. Peter). The agreement ceded all their lands north of the Minnesota River to the U.S. in exchange for a reservation along the Minnesota and annual payments of gold and food. In 1862, fed up with the U.S. government's failure to keep its end of the bargain, and starving because of drought and delayed shipment of supplies, they raided the agency, touching off a series of battles between the U.S. and Native Americans that lasted until the 1880s.

All that remains of the agency is the stone warehouse that the Indians raided in 1862. It's been restored by the Minnesota Historical Society and stands kitty-corner to an interpretive center. Walking trails take you down to the old Redwood Ferry landing along the Minnesota River where some fierce fighting took place. The site is administered by the Lower Sioux Indian Community. It may be closed for certain cultural observances. Call 507-697-6321 to make sure it's open.

The King of Trails South

Although US 75 runs 408 miles up Minnesota's spine, it was called the "King of Trails" 'way back before the trunk highway system was introduced in the 1920s. It really begins at Texas' Gulf Coast and splits the continent in two, ending in Winnipeg, Manitoba.

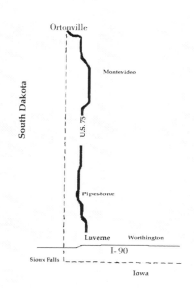

Luverne-Ortonville, 115 miles

Begin your ride in Luverne, population 4,600. Luverne is situated at the crossroads of US 75 and I-90 and is used to hosting bikers on their way to and from the annual Sturgis, South Dakota, motorcycle rally. Though not abundant, hotel rooms are more numerous here than in Pipestone.

While you're in Luverne, you can go sky-diving, take in a movie or play at the restored Palace Theatre, or visit the <u>Brandenburg Gallery</u>, 213 E. Luverne St., which features the photos and books of National Geographic photographer and Luverne native Jim Brandenburg. If you're hungry, you can more than satisfy your appetite at Sharkee's, 705 Kniss Avenue. The burgers are a full half pound.

I-90 provides a convenient entry onto US 75. The "King of Trails" is a two-lane blacktop road without a great deal of traffic. Ralph said the lack of other vehicles on the road made him feel as though we were traveling the wide-open spaces of the desert Southwest. In fact, the only life you may see is a hawk resting on a round hay bale and soaking up the warming rays of the morning sun. (It's a different story on the second weekend of September, when the King of Trails becomes a 414-mile marketplace of antiques and collectibles, fresh produce and baked goods.)

North of Luverne, signs on the right point to <u>Blue Mounds State Park</u>. Turn left at Rock Co. 20 and drive past a couple of farms to the park entrance. The park ranger will give you a map that shows you various hiking trails, parking spots, campsites and swimming beaches. It will also show you the bison viewing platform.

Bison at Blue Mounds State Park

The Blue Mounds is the only Minnesota state park that features a bison range, and it takes up a good share of the park's 1,800-plus acres. The herd is stable at about 100 head. The buffalo move around their range during the day, so if you don't see them at the viewing stand, you may see them as you walk along one of the trails. They're very skittish, dangerous critters—stay behind the fence.

The walk around the bison enclosure gives you a good idea of the type of territory our pioneer ancestors found when they came out here to homestead. In late summer prairie grasses reach seven feet to the sun, and wildflowers dance against the brilliant blue sky. Blue Mounds was never used for agricultural crops—the soil is too rocky. It was used as grazing land, however. The Minnesota Department of Natural Resources is working on restoring its native vegetation.

To get a totally different look at Blue Mounds, get back on your motorcycle and drive to the southern entrance off Co. Rd. 8. Quartzite cliffs rise out of the prairie. Early settlers thought they looked blue, hence the name. Although there are stories that the Native Americans used the cliffs to send buffalo hurtling to their deaths, no bison bones have ever been found at the base. Archaeologists have, however, found a strange, 1,250-foot alignment of rocks near the southern end of the park. It lines up perfectly with the sun during the spring and autumnal equinoxes. No one knows who built it.

After visiting the park, head back to US 75 and turn north.

In a matter of minutes you'll arrive in Pipestone, home of the ancient quarries where Native Americans still chip out catlinite to make pipes, amulets and jewelry. Much of the city has been built out of the dark rose Sioux quartzite that is native to the area. Stop by the Historic Calumet Inn, 104 W Main St , for lunch, or swing into Lange's, 110 8th Ave. S.E., for coffee and a piece of pie or a gigantic cinnamon roll.

It's just 19 miles from Pipestone to Lake Benton, but you'll soon find yourself in an area that's covered with wildflowers from spring to fall. They dance and toss their pretty heads in the ever-present prairie wind. The Hole-in-the-Mountain Prairie is a remnant of the original prairie that covered most of western Minnesota. It's administered by the Nature Conservancy, and is home to a rare species of butterfly, the Dakota skipper. Although you can't ride your motorcycle in the preserve, there is a turnout on the west side of Hwy. 75 where you can park your bike and walk in. It's free, but it's definitely a "look, but don't touch" place.

Back out on the highway, you'll spot some of the more than 600 wind turbines that line the Buffalo Ridge. Because of them, you'll know you're in Lake Benton long before you reach the intersection of Hwy. 75 and US 14 (also known as the Laura

Ingalls Wilder Historic Highway). Lake Benton is extremely proud of its wind power industry and bills itself as the "Original Wind Power Capital of the Midwest." For $2 per person, you can visit the Heritage and Wind Power Learning Center at 100 South Center St. and get a tour of the wind farm. Take a look, too, at the Lake Benton Opera House, which is on the National Register of Historic Places and presents live theatrical productions from March-December.

Prairie potholes become more numerous as you drive north. Round little bodies of water surrounded by reeds and cattails, they dot the landscape like a trail of muddy footprints. They're part of North America's most important areas for duck reproduction, and support more than half of the continent's migratory waterfowl.

In the midst of this avian paradise is the town of Madison, self-proclaimed "Lutefisk Capital of the World." Madison also has the distinction of being located on the 45th parallel, which means you're half-way to the North Pole (or the Equator, depending on your point of view). It is the birthplace of internationally-acclaimed poet Robert Bly who was named Minnesota's first Poet Laureate in 2008. Madison also boasts a Wissota Speedway. Races are held every Sunday evening from Memorial Day to Labor Day.

Just a mile south of Ortonville, a turnout on the west side of US 75 leads to the Big Stone National Wildlife Refuge. The 11,000-plus-acre refuge encompasses wetlands, rock formations and tallgrass prairie. A six-mile, self-guided auto tour route within the refuge allows you to stop and look at various types of wildlife habitat. The route is paved and is open from sunrise to dusk, May-September. The refuge is open from sunrise to sundown daily.

Resting at the southern tip of Big Stone Lake, Ortonville straddles Big Stone and Lac Qui Parle counties and is the county seat for Big Stone. During World War II the city was the site of a prisoner-of-war camp at the Big Stone Canning Company, now part of Dean Foods. Prisoners worked in the warehouse during the corn-canning season or shocked grain for local farmers.

Corn is still a big crop in the Ortonville area. On the third weekend of August the town hosts the Ortonville Cornfest at Lakeside Park. The event features a parade, chili cookoff and free corn on the cob.

If you can't wait for August, try the Matador Supper Club. It's right on US 75, and the locals swear by it.

The Southeast

The Land the Glaciers Forgot

When the glaciers pulled out of Minnesota some 10,000 to 12,000 years ago, they left a corner of the state behind. While the rest of the region was covered with silt, sand, clay, gravel and boulders ("drift"), this area was bypassed. Today, the "driftless" area is a

heady combination of limestone bluffs, hills, valleys, sinkholes and caves. The roads twist and turn on their way to the tops of the bluffs, and they perform the same maneuvers going down. It's a biker's paradise.

Apple Blossom Loop

Although the Apple Blossom Scenic Byway runs 17 miles from La Crescent to Nodine, this loop begins in La Crescent and ends in Dresbach, giving you a chance to ride the Historic Bluff County Scenic Byway (MN 16) or the Great River Road (US 61) while you're in the area. The best time of year to enjoy it may be early spring, when the blooming apple orchards have an ethereal, a fairyland appearance.

Quick Directions

US 61/14 south to La Crescent.
Right on S. 3rd St., 2 blocks.
Right on Houston Co. 29 (Elm St.)
Co. 29 becomes Winona Co. 1
Right at Winona Co. 12
Right at River St. in Dakota
Cross US 61/14
Right at Riverview Drive through Dresbach, back to US 61/14

Take US 61/14 south from Winona to La Crescent, known as Minnesota's "Apple Capital." At the intersection where 61 and 14 head east to LaCrosse, Wis., and MN 16 divides into an east-west route, make a right turn onto S. 3rd St.

Ride two blocks and turn right onto Houston Co. 29 (also known as Elm St.). You'll travel through a quiet residential area. As you pass La Crescent United Methodist church on your left, the road begins to climb. When you approach the edge of town, the name changes to N. Ridge Road and the road throws curves at you left and right.

At the top of the ridge, the road becomes Winona Co. 1 and is named the Apple Blossom Scenic Byway. It's a National Scenic Byway, designated by the U.S. Secretary of Transportation in 1995. Although the apple orchards are not as numerous as they once were, the remaining orchards put on a spectacular display on both sides of the road every spring when the trees are in bloom, and in late summer/early autumn when they yield crispy, tasty Minnesota apples.

An indicator of what's ahead on the Apple Blossom Byway

The road itself is nicely paved. With little traffic to worry about, the hills and curves are a biker's delight. The tops of the bluffs not only offer million-dollar views, but showcase some million-dollar homes as well (there must be money in the apple business!).

It's hard not to get caught up in the joy of the ride, but try to stop now and again to take in the long vistas at the top of the bluffs. Below, the Mississippi River winds its way to the Gulf of Mexico, dotted with islands and glittering in the sun. In the distance the bluffs on the Wisconsin side of the river beckon like cool, blue, misty mountains. It's some of Minnesota's best scenery.

Looking across the blufftops to Wisconsin.

Co. 1 ends at a T intersection with Co. 12. If you go to the left, the road will take you to Nodine, distinguished by St. John's Lutheran Church and School and a 30-foot-tall man made of drain tile that advertises Nodine Culvert Sales.

Take a right, and you'll immediately enter a series of S curves that wind you past the South Wind Orchard Reservoir. As you enter the town of Dakota (population 323 in 2010), Co. 12 takes on the additional name of Center St. At the intersection of Center and Riverview Drive is another T. There's an antique store to your right at the intersection.

A left turn keeps you on Co. 12 and leads to Ridgeway and Witoka. At Witoka, you can continue to ride MN 43 to Winona, or take Co.17 down Witoka Hill and past the Bridges Golf Course and Signatures restaurant into Winona. You can also catch Co. 9, which goes down into Cedar Valley, past the Cedar Valley Golf Course and terminates on US 61. (Caution: Portions of Co. 9 are crushed rock!)

We made a right turn onto Riverview and continued south. The railroad tracks streaming on the left side of the road belong to Amtrak. You may get a chance to race the Empire Builder, speeding on to Chicago. The race will be short-lived, however, as there are only 1.8 miles between Dakota and Dresbach. Then Co. 12 peters out, and you're back to US 61.

Brownsville Loop

Although this route is only a 32-mile round-trip, it had us feeling high for the rest of the day.

Quick Directions:

MN 26 South to Brownsville
Right on Houston Co. 14
Right on Houston Co. 5 to Caledonia
Right on Main Street (Houston Co. 3) back to Brownsville

Drive south from La Crescent to Brownsville via MN 26. Take time to stop at the Brownsville Overlook and check out the Upper Mississippi River Wildlife Refuge. The view of the river with its many little bays, islands, marshes and backwaters is beautiful, especially when the sunlight dances on the water. Via plaques, the U. S. Fish and Wildlife Service does a great job of explaining its mission to protect this unique area and its wildlife for future generations.

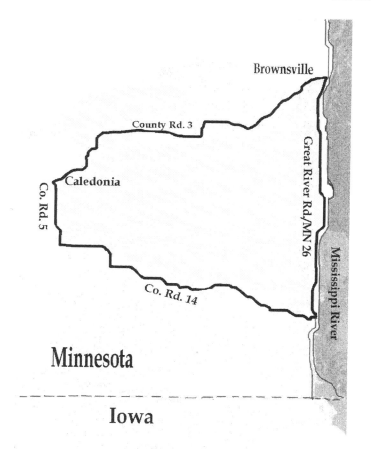

At Houston Co. Rd. 14, take a right. You will immediately begin an uphill drive that tops out on the bluffs above. The two-lane blacktop pavement is in good shape. The road is hilly, and it twists and turns around some of the most beautiful dairy farms in the state.

Black-and-white Holstein cows graze in lush green pastures. Cornfields are edged with blue chicory plants that seem to take their color directly from the sky. Many barns are decorated with 8-ft. by 8-ft. paintings of quilt designs.

The Barn Quilt project began in 2008. Now, more than sixty barns in Houston County now sport colorful designs with equally colorful names such as "Gentlemen's Fancy," "Windmill," and "Cottage Tulips." You can download driving directions with GPS coordinates for a blacktop-only quilt tour (many of the barns are on gravel roads) at www.visitcaledonia.com/barn_quilts.html.

As you fly along blufftops, you'll feel not only the wind, but a delicious sense of freedom. You can't help but grin.

When Co. 14 meets Co. 5, go right and drive toward Caledonia, Minnesota's "Wild Turkey Capital." Caledonia is also the county seat and home of the Houston County Fair, which is held in mid-August. If you're there at that time, you can take in a rodeo, demolition derby or tractor pull. When you reach Caledonia's Main Street, take a right. You'll travel through a residential area for a few blocks before hitting the open road again. You are now on Co. Rd. 3.

This road winds a little more leisurely through the country-side. There are more trees lining the road than along the bluff-top roads, giving the route a more intimate feel. As you near Brownsville, you will make a steep downhill run to an S-curve that shoots you northeastward into downtown Brownsville. At the end of the road, where Co. 3 meets MN 26, stop in at the Copper Penny, which sits at the foot of the bluff. It's favorite stop for bikers.

The Copper Penny is a favorite stop for bikers.

The Great River Road, Hwy. 61 South

Hwy. 61 is part of the Great River Roa, which begins at Lake Itasca and runs alongside the Mississippi River all the way through the middle of the country to New Orleans. High limestone bluffs loom over this section of the road, making it one of the most spectacular rides in Minnesota, particularly in the fall.

Quick Directions:

Hwy. 61 from Hastings to La Crescent
South on MN16
MN 26 to the Minnesota/Iowa border

Hastings to the Iowa line, 165 miles

This ride begins at the intersection of MN 55 and US 61 in Hastings, the first river town you'll encounter. Although soldiers from Fort Snelling camped there in 1820, settlement didn't actually begin until 1851. Alexis Bailly, Alexander Faribault and Henry Hastings Sibley were early developers of the region. The three put their names in a hat, and Hastings, Sibley's middle name, was the winning draw.

From the intersection, ride south on US 61 (Vermillion Street). Cross the Vermillion River at Dakota Co. Rd. 47 (Vermillion Rd). Vermillion Falls Park will be on your left, next to the oldest continuously operating flour mill in Minnesota, established in 1853.

As you near the Ford dealership on the south end of town, you have a choice to make. You can continue on 61, or take MN 316 (Red Wing Blvd.), which will bring you back to 61 just north of Red Wing. Traffic on this road is lighter than on 61.

If you continue south on 61, the name of the road changes from Vermillion Street to Lillehei Ave. at the edge of town. If you take a right at 180th St., you'll find signs pointing you to a dirt road and <u>Alexis Bailly Vineyard</u>, the oldest vineyard in Minnesota. Opened in 1978, its tasting room is open Friday, Saturday and Sunday from 11:00 a.m. to 5:00 p.m. The winery also hosts jazz concerts on Sundays during July and August, rain or shine.

Back on 61, at the intersection with 220th St., you'll see an old haybine adorned with a sign for the <u>Little Loghouse Pioneer Village</u>. Steve and Sylvia Bauer have made a habit of collecting old buildings and using them to re-create a village. From old churches to a scale replica of the old Hastings Spiral Bridge, they have preserved some priceless pieces of Americana. Their most recent acquisition was the legendary Porky's Diner from University Ave. in St. Paul. You can ride by the village any time. Once a year the Bauers open the gates for the Little Loghouse Antique Power Show, usually the last weekend in July.

From 220th, it's just a short ride to the intersection with MN 50, where 61 takes a left. The pavement between Hastings and Red Wing is bumpy. The road is two-lane leaving Hastings, but widens to four lanes as you approach Red Wing.

Miesville, population 125, lies between the two. If you're hungry, stop into King's Place for a cheap burger—you have 54 kinds to choose from. If the Miesville Mudhens are playing baseball in the field across the street, however, you might have to stand in line. The bar and grill are open 11:00 a.m. 10:00 p.m. Tuesday through Saturday.

As Hwy. 61 winds closer to the Mississippi, the scenery shifts from flat cornfields to towering bluffs. You'll see the first limestone outcroppings before you cross the Cannon River into Red Wing.

Red Wing gets its name from an Indian chief named Hupahuduta, who met explorer Zebulon Pike in the area in 1805. Hupahuduta carried a swan's wing, dyed red, to indicate his status as chief. The city of Red Wing has grown to become one of Minnesota's manufacturing centers and is the home of Red Wing Shoes (work boots), Riedell Shoes (ice and roller skates) and BIC pens and advertising specialties.

Although the Internet has caused many antiques dealers to go out of business, Red Wing still hosts a number of antique shops which sell a good deal of Red Wing pottery. There are several good restaurants in town, and the St. James Hotel, 406 Main Street, is a posh place to eat, shop and stay. Many of the city's grand Victorian homes have been converted to bed-and-breakfast establishments.

As you cruise through the heart of Red Wing, you'll see Barn Bluff at what looks like the end of the road. Never fear, 61 takes a curve to the right at the foot of the 350-ft. bluff. There are hiking trails up to the summit, with stairs leading the first quarter of the way (a parking lot is nearby). You may be somewhat breathless at the top, but the view is well worth the climb. You may see hawks, falcons and eagles soar over the river as tugboats churn their way through the water below.

Hwy. 61 is a two-lane road running south out of Red Wing. As you travel south, limestone bluffs rise more frequently along the river, and at times you ride along the backwaters of Ole Miss.

It's just ten miles from Red Wing to Frontenac, which is actually two communities in one. Frontenac Station is located on Hwy. 61; further east is Old Frontenac, where the entire community, which includes many Civil War-era homes, is on the National Register of Historic Places. In between is Frontenac State Park which overlooks the 25,000-acre wide spot in the Mississippi known as Lake Pepin.

Lake Pepin is home to the waterfront town of Lake City, the "birthplace of water-skiing." It was here in 1922 that Ralph Samuelson strapped a couple of barrel staves to his feet and had someone drag him around the lake behind a boat. That experiment lead to the use of snow skis, and finally a pair of water skis he made himself. The rest is history.

Today you can waterski, fish or sail on Lake Pepin. You can also rent a houseboat. The mom-and-pop motels that used to line Hwy. 61 are being replaced by condominiums that you can rent by the day, the week or longer. Lake City has a number of good restaurants, and their owners are accustomed to serving bikers. Lake City can be crowded on weekends. Watch out for bicyclists on the shoulders as you ride through town.

The highway hugs the river a little tighter as you cruise south toward Camp Lacupolis which sits down below the highway, along the deepest part of Lake Pepin. The bluffs crowd the highway, and the road twists and turns as you near the village of Reads Landing. At one time it boasted 27 hotels as well as several churches, bars and warehouses.

It's a mere three miles from Reads Landing to Wabasha. The highway widens to four lanes as you near the "Home of Grumpy Old Men." It was here, in 1993, that Jack Lemmon, Walter Matthau and Ann-Margaret filmed portions of "Grumpy Old Men" and made ice-fishing look like fun. One of the places mentioned in the movie is Slippery's Bar & Restaurant, 10 Church Ave. "Grumpy" and "Grumpier" play continuously on the big-screen TV, but a better reason to go there is to sit on the deck, which is right on the water, and watch the river traffic as you enjoy your meal. Wabasha has many other restaurants worth trying.

Wabasha, named after the third Dakota chief of that name, is also home to the <u>National Eagle Center</u>, 50 Pembroke St. The non-profit center puts on demonstrations with live bald eagles at 11:00 a.m., 1:00 and 3:00 p.m. daily, March through October. These eagles were found injured in the wild and rehabilitated, but are unable to survive on their own. Admission is \$8 for adults. You can also watch eagles in the wild from the center's riverside deck. Wabasha is known as a favorite eagle nesting and hunting area.

As you drive along Hwy. 61, beware of "bluff gawkers," people who slow down to crane their necks at the bluffs above them. You may cruising along at 65 mph and suddenly find yourself on the bumper of a car that's slowed down to 30. The sides of the road and the median are thick with wildflowers in midsummer. Sky-blue chicory, black-eyed Susans, red clover and wild parsnip put on a bright, sweet-smelling display.

From Wabasha the highway is four lanes wide. It sweeps you through Kellogg, Weaver, Minneiska and Minnesota City before delivering you to Winona, named for Wenonah, the first-born daughter of Chief Wabasha.

Winona is a college town and gaining a reputation for the arts as well. In the summer, it hosts the Great River Shakespeare Festival and the Minnesota Beethoven Festival. <u>The Minnesota Marine Art Museum</u>, 800 Riverview Drive, is open from 10:00 a.m. to 5:00 p.m. Tuesday through Sunday and features art "inspired by water," including a Van Gogh, as well as several Hudson River School painters.

One of the most recognizable landmarks in Winona is the Sugar Loaf, an 85-ft. rocky bluff that stands by itself at the junction of US 61 and MN 43. River pilots thought it resembled sugar, which used to be sold in cones. According to Dakota legend, it was once part of a mountain that two Dakota villages fought over.

The Great Spirit ended the argument by dividing the mountain, leaving Barn Bluff in Red Wing and moving the Sugar Loaf to Winona. A large piece of the bluff broke off in 2004.

Hwy. 61 remains a four-lane highway south of Winona. After it passes through the town of Dakota, 61 runs concurrently with US 14 and I-90. I-90 turns to cross the river toward LaCrosse just before reaching La Crescent. Expect to hit some rather hard, irregular bumps in the concrete near LaMoille.

Rivulets of water stain the banded limestone walls of the surrounding bluffs as you continue south on 61 to La Crescent, Minnesota's "Apple Capital." In the middle of the city, Hwy. 61 turns left to continue its downriver journey through Wisconsin.

The Great River Road offers spectacular vistas of the Mississippi River.

You can remain on the Minnesota side of the river by taking MN 16 south. When 16 begins to bend to the west, take MN 26 south. Pull over near Brownsville at the overlook for the Upper

Mississippi River Wildlife Refuge. The refuge protects 240,000 acres of the Mississippi River floodplain from Wabasha to Illinois. It's a watery tangle of sloughs, swamps and islands inhabited by bald eagles, swans, lake sturgeon and American eels, deer and several species of ducks.

The last inhabited place on MN26 in Minnesota is Reno. The road runs past it to New Albin, Iowa.

Worth a Visit:

If you want to feel like a kid again, visit <u>Lark Toys</u>, right on Hwy. 61 in Kellogg. Baby boomers will recognize the toys of their youth from Howdy Doody marionettes to little green army men. The building also houses a candy store, an ice cream shop, a bookstore and a mini golf course outdoors. But the biggest attraction is the hand-made carousel. It was designed by former owner Donn Kreofsky and carved and painted by local artists. It costs just $2 to ride the fanciful animals on the carousel.

Best Lunch!

Reads Landing Brewing Company

Just down the hill from Hwy. 61 in Reads Landing, is Reads Landing Brewing Company, which can only be described as a "find." Located on the river (with only an occasional Amtrak or freight train passing in front of it), this restaurant has ambiance, designated motorcycle parking and good food!

A former dry goods store built in 1869, the building was used as a restaurant from the 1930s to the 1950s, then as a family "cabin." Scott Tisland, who learned the fine dining business at Vincent in Minneapolis and at Ray's on the River in Atlanta, is the chef.

Even a humble chicken salad sandwich is something to celebrate. The bread is fresh. Instead of wallowing in mayonnaise, the chicken and toasted almonds are laid neatly down on the bread with just a swipe of mayo over the top of the bread. The sweet potato tots are incredible! Ralph had the wild rice brat, hand made by Burts Meats in Eyota. The restaurant also features a full list of craft beers, some made in nearby Rollingstone, Minn.

Minnesota Hwy. 43

Quick Directions

MN 43 north
Left on Fillmore Co. 18
Left on Fillmore Co. 12
Right on Fillmore Co. 23
Right on Fillmore Co. 10
MN 43 north
I-90 east for 7 miles
MN 43 north to Winona

We thought MN 43 looked like an interesting way to get back to Winona. A detour made it even more enjoyable.

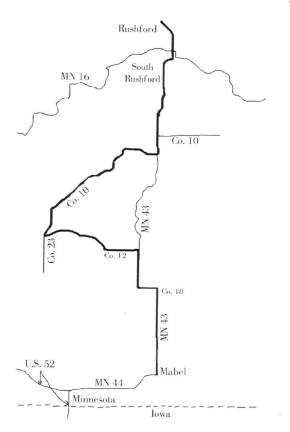

Mabel to Rushford

We caught MN 43 at its intersection with MN 44 in Mabel which bills itself as "America's Steam Engine Capital." The town was named for a little girl named Mabel, the daughter of the town's postmaster back in the late 1800s. We'd come from nearby Harmony, and the road between the two towns had a weird, striped patch job running along it. Ralph couldn't decide which part of the road was the least bumpy—the patched surface or the unpatched asphalt. On 43 now, the pavement was smooth as we angled northeast toward Winona.

Seven miles north of town, the highway takes a jog to the west where it meets Fillmore Co. 18. At the end of the jog, however, 43

129

was blocked, and we were told to detour along Co. 12. The frothy flowers of Queen Anne's Lace, a wild cousin of the carrot, edged the fields in white. There were few tractors and combines visible. At an old white farmhouse, wood smoke curled up from the chimney, even though it was July, and the temperature was in the 90s. We were in Amish country, and an Amish mama was baking bread for her family.

The road began to curl and curve, and we swooped up hills and down. At the intersection of Co. 12 and Co. 23, we were directed to turn to the right. We were on an amusement park ride filled with hills and curves and had no idea where the ride would end. Ralph found it helpful to keep the Victory in fourth gear, instead of than downshifting all the time.

Somewhere in the middle of Fillmore County, 23 branched off to the left and we found ourselves on Co. 10. We zoomed through a wide spot in the road called Highland where the Highland Lutheran Church is the main attraction. After passing the church, the highway turned to the left. We saw some beautiful orange-red limestone outcroppings, then found ourselves in another small place, Bratsberg, which appeared to be a collection of farm buildings. We also met up with MN 43 again.

MN 43 near Bratsberg

We turned left and drove north through Rushford. We crossed into Winona County, passed St. Johns Cemetery—a well-kept spot carved out of the neighboring cornfields—and came upon another once-upon-a-town, Hart. It consisted of some farm buildings and St. Johns Church.

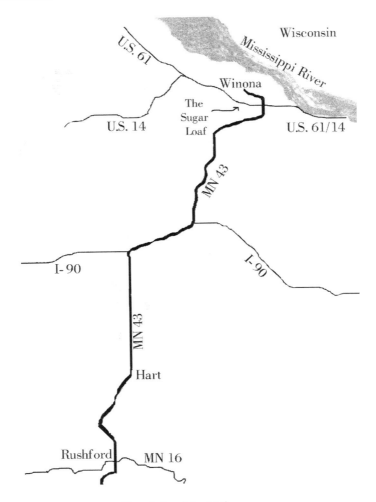

Rushford to Winona

About five miles up the road, we met I-90 and had no alternative but to get on the freeway and continue east. Seven miles later, the MN 43 exit appeared, and we took it.

MN 43 continued to give us curves and glimpses of the limestone beneath the hills all the way to Winona. We entered the city on a downhill run under the sentinel-like presence of the Sugar Loaf bluff. It was a hot, 105-degree day, and our air-conditioned hotel room was a welcome haven.

Historic Bluff Country Scenic Byway, Minnesota Hwy. 16

Hokah to Dexter, 88 miles

Whether you travel east to west or vice-versa, this is one of the best rides in the state.

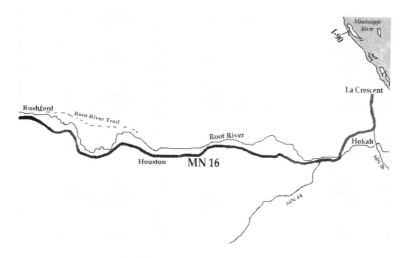

La Crescent to Rushford

"Wow!," Ralph exclaimed as we settled into a booth at <u>Pedal Pushers</u> in Lanesboro. "That was a ride!"

We had finished riding the Apple Blossom Loop earlier in the morning and decided to take MN 16 west. Designated a national scenic byway in 2002, the Historic Bluff Country Scenic Byway truly lives up to its name. It passes through many historic towns as it winds through southeastern Minnesota and provides sights you won't find elsewhere in the state.

The journey began at the intersection of US 61 and MN 16, south of Winona. We followed the signs that pointed us to Hokah. Named after Chief Wecheschatope Hokah, this little town—whose total area is only .7 mile—is neatly tucked in between Thompson Creek Bluff (known locally as Mt. Tom) and the Root River. The area features the Mound Prairie Scientific and Natural Area, where you can find rare plant and animal species along nature trails.

The highway is a smooth two-lane. Because you're starting out in the bottom of a river valley, there are no hills to climb. But there are curves, lots of gentle, gliding curves.

As we neared Houston, the curves became more frequent. Crops in the broad river valley alternated between corn and soybeans as the tall limestone bluffs stood guard. The Root River flowed alongside us, headed in the opposite direction to meet the Mississippi River. A bluff on the north side of the town proclaims the town's presence in big white letters: "HOUSTON." It was built by Civilian Conservation Corps members in the 1930s as a landmark for small aircraft pilots.

High bluffs surround cornfields near Houston.

Houston was also once the home of Cody, the buffalo. A bison with a gentle disposition and a taste for Oreo cookies, Cody portrayed himself in *Dances With Wolves*. He also modeled for the buffalo head nickel issued by the U.S. Treasury in 2005. He died the following year at the Money Creek Buffalo Ranch in Houston at the age of 19. The nearby Houston Nature Center is a great place to learn about area wildlife; it holds an International Festival of Owls the first weekend in March (check the weather before biking to it!).

The Root River Bike Trail begins in Houston. It was once a railroad line, and it runs alongside MN 16 up to Lanesboro and over to Preston. It's one of the most popular bike trails in Minnesota. On weekends, you'll see crowds of cyclists on the path.

The terrain became more hilly as we left Houston.

At Rushford Village, the road takes a turn to the right and joins MN 43. We rode over the bridge (S. Mill St.) into downtown Rushford, where MN 16 passes the Creamery restaurant before turning west. If you get a chance, stop in at Norsland Lefse, 210 West Jessie St. It's the first mechanized lefse factory in the U. S., and you can watch that Norwegian delicacy being made—with real potatoes! (They sell delicious muffins, donuts and sweet rolls, and tools for making lefse at home, too.)

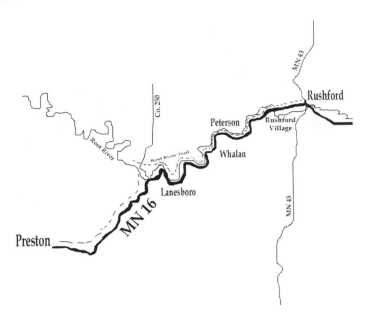

Rushford to Preston

The Root River snakes its way through the countryside, its blue-green waters filled with pools for trout. In early spring, the bottomlands between Rushford and Peterson are covered with a lake of sky-blue Virginia bluebells.

It's a curvy, uphill ride from Peterson to Lanesboro. The curves vary from quick to long, and the countryside is lush and green. Limestone bluffs tower over you, and the land has an almost mystical, medieval feeling to it.

If you feel inclined, take a quick detour to the right to Whalan, population 50. This little dot on the map is famous for two things— pie, and the Stand-Still Parade, which is held the third Saturday in May. At this parade, the parade units stand still in the middle of town and the audience walks around it.

One more uphill push, and you're in Lanesboro, named one of 100 Best Small Art Towns in America by author John Vilani and one of 50 Best Outdoor Sports Towns by *Sports Afield* magazine (take your pick). The town took early advantage of its proximity to the Root River Trail and has become a major tourism destination. You'll find many bed-and-breakfast establishments, live theater, and lots of shopping and dining experiences. You can also take guided tours into Amish country (Fillmore County has the largest concentration of Old Order Amish in Minnesota), or go tubing on the Root River. The town is motorcycle-friendly.

A parade of inner tubers crosses the street in Lanesboro.

You could spend a lot of time and money in Lanesboro, but there's still a lot of Hwy. 16 to be explored. As we drove uphill out of Lanesboro, we were on the alert for Amish farmers. There is a Farmers Market in town on Saturdays, and it's not uncommon to see their black buggies slowly descending the steep, winding curve into town.

The next town on MN 16 is Preston, self-proclaimed Trout Capital of Minnesota and home to the National Trout Center.

(There's a large trout next to the visitors information booth to reinforce that idea.) It's also the place where the Root River Trail and the Harmony-Preston Valley State Bike Trail meet. If you're looking for a good steak dinner, the <u>Branding Iron Supper Club</u> atop the hill at the junction of MN 16 and US 52, can supply it.

As we left Preston, the terrain along MN 16 began to change. The hills and curves gradually disappeared, replaced by open prairie and wind farms.

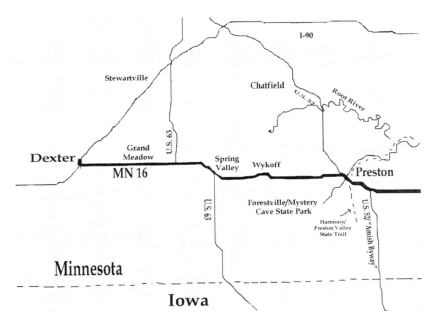

At the intersection of MN 16 and Fillmore Co. 11, we saw signs for Forestville and Mystery Cave State Park. Forestville was bypassed by the railroad in 1868 and by 1890 the entire town was owned by one man. The village's fifty residents worked for housing, boarding and store credit. Forestville, in the middle of the park, has been preserved by the Minnesota Historical Society. Mystery Cave is also in the park and the Minnesota Department of Natural Resources offers everything from scenic tours to wild caving tours. Find out about them at the park entrance.

The closest town to Forestville along MN 16 is Wykoff. This town's primary claim to fame is Ed's Museum, which includes an authentic 1930-40s Jack Sprat Food Store, and the Wykoff Schools Museum, which displays memorabilia from 1897 to 1992. If you've never spent a night in jail, you can in Wykoff, at the Jail Haus Bed & Breakfast.

Spring Valley is next. The Methodist Church Museum, 221 West Courtland St., is a Laura Ingalls Wilder site (Laura married Almanzo Wilder here).If you're a fan of the *Little House* books, you may want to visit. Spring Valley is also the boyhood home of Richard Sears, founder of Sears & Roebuck.

Deer Creek Speedway is located in Spring Valley. You can watch four classes of Wissota racing cars and two USRA modified classes there Saturdays from April to September. Check www. deercreekspeedway.com for the complete schedule.

The road from Spring Valley to Grand Meadow is straight as an arrow but extremely bumpy. The pavement gives you a jolt every 16 feet. It probably hasn't seen a paving crew in ten years! The bumps continue all the way to Dexter where the byway ends. The Windmill Travel Plaza, with its iconic windmill, is a fitting punctuation point to a beautiful ride.

Worth a Stop:

Pedal Pushers, 121 Parkway Ave. N., Lanesboro, offers up fresh, locally-produced foods. The hamburgers are made from grass-fed beef, and pies are topped with local pasteurized whipped cream. Another good eatery is Riverside on the Root, 109 S. Parkway. Here you can dine on everything from sandwiches to chipotle pork chops. You can also enjoy a late-night martini, or rent an inner tube and go floating down the Root River!

Shooting Star Scenic Byway, MN 56

Named for one of the wildflowers found along the route, the Shooting Star Scenic Byway is one of the shorter scenic byways in Minnesota, just 26 miles long. Nevertheless, it's a pleasant ride.

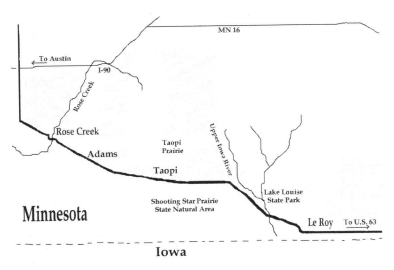

Rose Creek to Le Roy, 26 Miles

We picked up the Shooting Star off I-90, near Austin, although you may want to start at the other end, at the junction of US 63 and MN 56 near Le Roy.

The ride down along MN 56 was quiet after the rush of the freeway traffic. Grasshoppers and cicadas sang in the roadside ditches. The two-lane blacktop angled toward the southeast as we approached the town of Rose Creek.

The town was incorporated in 1899, although there has been a post office there since 1865. Rose Creek, a tributary of the Cedar

River, flows through the town. It's a peaceful little place where you can get a tap beer at Woody's Bar and Grill for a buck. The Rose Pedaler offers a comfortable night's stay in its three-suite log cabin. Or just stop in for an ice cream cone.

It's a mere eight miles from Rose Creek to Adams. The Shooting Star Byway was designated in 1994. Its purpose is to protect and preserve remnants of the tallgrass prairie which once grew here. The Minnesota Department of Natural Resources and local fire crews ignite prescribed burns along the byway to keep the weeds down and the wildflowers growing. Along the way, I spied the midsummer black-eyed Susans, purple coneflowers, and bright pink blazing stars. The shooting stars for which the byway is named appear in the spring.

MN 56 follows the route of the old Chicago, Milwaukee and St. Paul Railroad which played a major role in the settlement of this part of Minnesota. The railroad bed has been paved with asphalt and is now the Shooting Star Trail. Although there were no bicyclists on it the day we passed by, it is expected to grow in popularity and will someday reach Austin and Lyle.

It's another eight miles from Adams to Taopi. The town is named after a Dakota man who was one of the first converts to Christianity at the Redwood mission on the Minnesota River. Taopi ("Wounded Man") was sympathetic to white settlers during the U.S.-Dakota conflict in 1862 and helped many of them to safety.

The town of Taopi was originally built next to a flour mill on the Wapsipinicon River. It was the largest steam-powered flour mill in southern Minnesota and could process 300,000 bushels of wheat a year. The mill was dismantled and moved to Janesville in 1877.

MN 56 showed us some gentle curves as we sped along. The pavement was neither rough nor smooth. The bike trail on the right was dotted with clumps of mauve Joe Pye Weed, bright yellow woodland sunflowers and lavender bee balm. One of the curves drew us over a bridge across the Upper Iowa River and into Le Roy, the last—and largest—town on the byway.

It's an agricultural community, as evidenced by the feed, seed and other ag-related businesses that line the main drag. Like Taopi, Le Roy was once a milling community. When the railroad built its tracks across the prairie, however, the town moved south toward the tracks. The mill ceased operation, and the family who owned the land around the millpond donated the property to the state of Minnesota. It was the beginning of Lake Louise State Park. The park offers swimming, fishing and camping and a peaceful place to rest after a day on the road, Memorial Day through Labor Day.

If your idea of "roughing it" veers more toward clean sheets and a hot meal, check out Sweet's Hotel, 128 W. Main St. The eight-suite hotel was built in 1898 by a veteran of the Civil War and is said to be haunted by friendly ghosts. The restaurant serves breakfast, lunch and dinner.

The road's siren call was loud for us, so we rode on through Le Roy. At the eastern edge of town, the pavement was new, smooth and straight. It led us right to US 63, where we turned left toward Rochester.

Minnesota Hwy. 55

Hastings to Tenney, 221 miles

MN 55 begins on the corner of 8th Street West and Vermillion Street (also known as US 61) in Hastings and ends without fanfare 220 miles later on the Minnesota-North Dakota border. Watch the landscape evolve from rural to urban and back again as you cross the state from east to west.

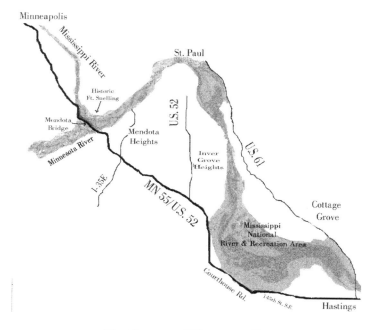

Hastings to Minneapolis

You'll start out with the Hastings High School football stadium on your right as you point your bike west and climb uphill past the shopping centers on the outskirts of town. As you pass the Dakota County Government Center and the sprawling Wal-Mart next to it, 8th Street is renamed 145th E. and Hastings Trail. Emerald Greens Golf Course will be on your left and farm fields begin to appear as the trail bends toward the northwest and is renamed Courthouse Blvd.

Flint Hills Resources' Pine Bend Refinery will come into view on your left. You may smell the gas being flared off as 55 joins MN 52 and makes a beeline toward the Twin Cities. Warehouses and distribution centers line the right side of the road as you pass through Inver Grove Heights. The highways split before the I-494 interchange, with MN 52 heading due north into downtown St. Paul and MN 55 angling northwest toward Mendota.

At the intersection of 55 and Lone Oak Road, you'll see a local landmark, Trinity Lone Oak Lutheran Church and School. The church was organized in 1881. Its first building on the site burned to the ground; the present church was built in 1901. The church and the road are named after a single bur oak that stood on the property for 115 years. Traffic, pollution and old age brought the great tree down in 1983. A cross section of it is preserved in Eagan's City Hall.

Hwy. 55 passes beneath the I-494 interchange and is joined briefly by MN 13 before it reaches the Minnesota River and the Mendota Bridge. When it was finished in 1926, the Mendota Bridge was the longest continuous concrete arch bridge in the world. Its thirteen arches span the river bottoms, and make a graceful connection between the southeastern suburbs and Minneapolis. At 4,113 feet, it's nearly a mile long and carries 39,000 cars per day.

It's dedicated to the "Gopher Gunners" of the 151st Field Artillery, who died in World War I and was placed on the National Register of Historic Places in 1979.

When you cross the bridge, you'll see the bottomlands of the Minnesota River as it nears its confluence with the Mississippi, and Fort Snelling State Park. The Minneapolis skyline is off in the distance to your right. Move a little closer to Minneapolis, and Historic Fort Snelling comes into view right below the MN 5 interchange.

MN 62 (Crosstown Hwy.) joins MN 55 on the left just after the interchange. You're in Hennepin County now. To stay on MN 55, keep to the right. Take the Hiawatha Avenue exit. Hiawatha has four lanes, two in each direction. It runs alongside Minnesota's first light rail line, the Hiawatha Line, which began operations in 2004. Traffic can be heavy, depending on the time of day.

As you cruise along the Hiawatha industrial district, you'll come to the Martin Olav Sabo bridge just north of Lake Street. A bike and pedestrian bridge, it's the first cable-stayed suspension bridge in Minnesota—and very nearly the last. This sculptural piece of architecture looks like a clipper ship under full sail and is very dramatic when it's lit at night. In February, 2012, some of the cable stays snapped, and the City of Minneapolis rushed to place scaffolding beneath the bridge. The bridge was closed for three months for repairs.

Beyond the bridge are the entrances to I-94 and I-35W. If you take the I-94 exit, you'll pass through downtown and the Lowry Hill tunnel, catching up with Hwy. 55 on the north side of the city, near the Minneapolis Farmers Market. Take the Lyndale Ave. N. exit and drive north to Olson Memorial Hwy. Go left to go west on MN 55.

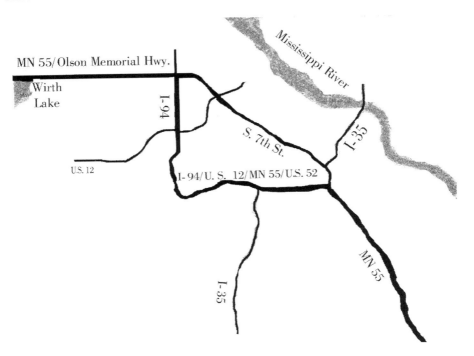

Hwy. 55 in downtown Minneapolis

You can take a slower (30 mph), more scenic route through downtown Minneapolis if you like. From Hiawatha, ignore both the I-94 and I-35W exits and ride straight into the city via the 7th Street exit.

As you roll into downtown, you'll be greeted by a three-block stretch of old brick churches and rough pavement. Fortunately, 7th is a one-way street heading west, so you don't have to worry about people making left turns from the opposite direction.

The pavement smoothes out just before you reach the triple-decker skyway of the Hennepin County Medical Center (HCMC) and the financial district's skyscrapers. Be on the lookout for bikes, pedestrians and pedicabs, especially around the Nicollet Mall. Watch out, too, for buses, which have the right of way, and may swing into traffic at any time.

After you cross Hennepin Ave., the First Avenue nightclub, where Prince filmed *Purple Rain,* will be on your left. The white stars on its black exterior walls bear the names of the artists who have performed there, including B.B. King, Marilyn Manson, and U2, to name a few. As 7th makes a slight hook to the west, Target Center, home of the Minnesota Timberwolves and Minnesota Lynx basketball teams, will be on your right. A block away, Target Field, the Minnesota Twins' much-lauded baseball stadium, will also appear on your right.

Continue up the hill to Olson Memorial Hwy. and take a left. Hwy. 55 was named after Minnesota Governor Floyd B. Olson, who served from 1931-1936. The son of Norwegian immigrants, he grew up in North Minneapolis. One of his major accomplishments was the introduction of a progressive income tax in the state of Minnesota (thanks, Floyd). His statue stands alongside the highway in the neighborhood in which he was raised.

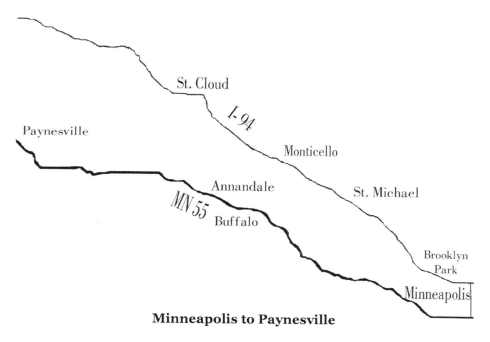

Minneapolis to Paynesville

As you leave downtown Minneapolis, MN 55 is a four-lane street divided by a grassy median. The median tapers and disappears by the time you reach the city limits and Wirth Lake. The highway divides the lake; it's not uncommon to see folks fishing from the pier on the southern portion. The road continues to stretch out to the west, through Golden Valley, Plymouth and into the exurbs of Hamel, Medina and Greenfield.

When you enter Rockford, you enter Wright County. The highway narrows to two lanes in this area. It's horse country, but even folks who don't own horses have white fences around their McMansions. The area is dotted with small ponds and lakes, and the Crow River twists its way amongst the gently rolling hills.

You might be tempted to stop for breakfast or lunch in Maple Lake. Don't bother. We cruised its entire, cute, downtown and found no eating establishments whatsoever. (Well, maybe the American Legion serves food, but it was too early for a beer!)

Buffalo is the next town up the highway. If you're an antiques maven, it's a great place to browse, with regular shops and frequent "occasional" sales offering a wide and interesting selection.

The road between Buffalo and Annandale gives you a bumpy ride. If you're traveling on a Saturday, be on the lookout for farm auctions. You'll recognize them by the long lines of pickup trucks parked along the shoulders. You may need to slow down to get past the traffic running in and out of the farm gates.

We crossed the North Fork of the Crow River and stopped for a late breakfast at the Homestyle Country Café, just off the highway at 95 Elm St. E. in Annandale. The food, as promised, is cooked from scratch. I ordered the special omelet which included potatoes. Breakfast became lunch as we waited for the cook to boil the potatoes so they could be cut up and fried before being put into the eggs. Our waitress apologized profusely for the delay and sent us on our way with a gigantic cinnamon roll that we shared the following morning.

We set out again, stopping for gas at Kimball where a concrete statue of a rooster informed us that broasted chicken was the specialty of the restaurant next to the station.

As we approached Eden Valley, we encountered an amazing sight, the Amaz'n Farmyard. The family-friendly amusement park lets you get up close and personal with thirty farm animals, get lost in a maze, bounce in the barn and ride down a 150-ft. slide that looks like it will dump you right out on the highway. We found the hills and curves on the highway more interesting.

The highway pulls you along through Meeker and Stearns counties, all the while paralleling I-94 to the north. MN 4 joins 55 shortly before you reach Paynesville and branches off to the north on the other side.

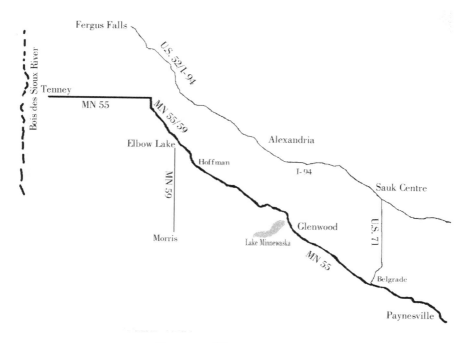

Paynesville to Tenney

The road between Paynesville and Elbow Lake quickly became Ralph's favorite part of this ride. With a series of gentle hills and pretty little curves, it's far prettier than the concrete ribbons of the interstate.

When we reached Glenwood, we pulled off of MN 55 to head downhill into downtown Glenwood. The <u>Lakeshore Steak and Chop House</u> stands invitingly on the shores of Lake Minnewaska. A popular destination, it serves up sizzling steaks and offers gorgeous views of the lake from its decks.

After dinner or a cool drink, we suggest a stroll down to the statue of the Indian woman, Minnewaska. The name of the statue by sculptor Linda Egle is "She Who Waits," and depicts a faithful woman awaiting the homecoming of her long-overdue lover. *Minnewaska* is actually a Dakota word meaning "good water." Glenwood holds is annual "Waterama" on Lake Minnewaska every July, with everything from senior-citizen bed races to waterski shows.

If you can pull yourself away from the water, get back on MN 55 and head toward Kensington. The town is near the farm where the Kensington Runestone was discovered. The stone, which some say is a record of a Viking expedition to Minnesota in the 1300s, is on display in Alexandria.

The pavement between Glenwood and Elbow Lake is smooth. You may see squadrons of pelicans flying from lake to lake in this area, and egrets fishing in shallow waters along the road. A rail line runs parallel to the highway as you travel from Pope County to Grant County; Ralph marveled at the roadbed's absolute straightness and accuracy.

If state boundaries were set according to terrain and not political agreements, Minnesota would end on the west side of Elbow Lake.

As you enter the town, you come upon a beautiful body of water, Flekkefjord Lake. Surrounded by trees on the hillsides, it's reminiscent of a Norwegian fjord. Hwy. 55 bends through the town and you meet Flekkefjord Lake again on the west end. This time, the terrain is concrete-slab flat. Farm fields stretch to the horizon. Although it's still 33 miles to the Minnesota-North Dakota border, you feel as if you've already crossed the state line.

From here on out, the towns get smaller. Tenney, the last Minnesota town on MN 55, consists of a few buildings and a line of grain bins along the highway. It looks more like a farm than a village.

The Bois des Sioux River is the end of the line.

As you near the end of your ride, you'll cross US 75. When you reach the bridge at the Bois des Sioux River, you've reached the end of Minnesota. Next stop, Fairmount, N.D.

Worth a Visit

Historic Fort Snelling

Although it's almost at the beginning of the ride, Historic Fort Snelling is a place you don't want to miss! Built in the early 1820s, this little triangle of land at the confluence of the Minnesota and Mississippi Rivers has played an important and enduring part in Minnesota history, from the fur trade through the Civil War and into World War II. Costumed re-enactors bring the old days to life. They may admire your leathers, but will give you a blank stare if you mention your motorcycle or bike. The fort is open Tuesday-Saturday, Memorial Day-Labor Day. Visit www. historicfortsnelling.org for hours and admission fees.

Re-enactors drill at Historic Ft. Snelling

Twin Cities-Hastings-Red Wing-Cannon Falls Loop,

138 miles

After a long, confining Minnesota winter, the urge to get outdoors and ride is overwhelming. Time to get your riding muscles back in shape! Ease back into life on the road with this little day trip.

Quick Directions

I-94 east through St. Paul
US 61 south to Hastings
Left at MN 50/US 61 to Miesville
Right at Goodhue Co. 7 (Co. 7 Blvd.)
West on MN 19 to Cannon Falls
Follow 19 to Main St.
Main St. to 4th St. (MN 20)
MN 20 back to Hastings

Take I-94 east out of downtown St. Paul. Along the way, you'll catch glimpses of the Minnesota State Capitol on your left, with its shining golden "Quadriga" horses-and-chariot statue. The Minnesota History Center will be on your right.

As you leave downtown and pass through Mounds Park near the Warner Road intersection and under Dayton's Bluff, you'll see some fine old houses atop the hill. Near Lower Afton Road, Pigs Eye Lake will appear on your right. It's named after "Pig's Eye" Parrant, the first European settler in the St. Paul area, who made his living selling whiskey to the Indians, starting around 1838.

Get into the right lane to take US 61 south as it splits from I-94. Hwy. 61 takes you through the cities of Newport, St. Paul Park and Cottage Grove. The scenery will become progressively more rural as you near Hastings.

A curve and steep hill give you a beautiful view of Hastings across the Mississippi River before you swoop down to the bottom lands and marinas that form a gateway to Hastings. Cross the river on the blue bridge, built in 1951. It's actually the second bridge to cross the river in Hastings. The first was a Spiral Bridge that served as a local landmark for many years. You still find businesses in Hastings with "spiral" in their names.

After the collapse of the I-35W bridge in downtown Minneapolis in 2007, the 1951 bridge was thoroughly examined and determined to be near the end of its life. A new bridge with a 100-year life expectancy is under construction and is expected to be completed in 2014.

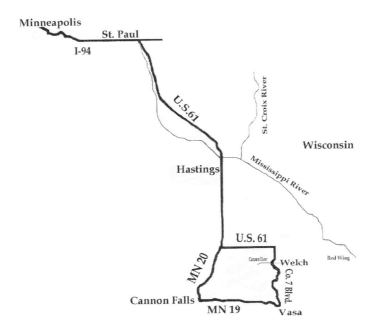

The claim for a township site in the Hastings area was made in 1851 by four veteran fur traders who played prominent roles in Minnesota history: Alexis Bailly; his son, Henry Bailly; Henry Hastings Sibley; and Alexander Faribault. The name of the town was drawn out of a hat, and Sibley's middle name was chosen. He later became the first governor of the state of Minnesota.

Hastings is chock-full of places that are on the National Register of Historic Sites, many of them downtown, where you'll find antique and jewelry shops to explore, art galleries to enjoy, and restaurants to dine in. Ample public parking is available. Turn left off of Hwy. 61 at Second Street to explore Hastings on foot.

Hwy. 61 becomes Vermillion Street in Hastings, and you'll see many historic homes along the way. The most prominent is the LeDuc House at 1629 Vermillion; it was once the home of distinguished Civil War officer, attorney and U.S. Agriculture Secretary William LeDuc. The home is open for tours from the end of May to the end of October. Check http://www.dakotahistory.org/LeDuc/home for hours and admission fees.

Continue south on Vermillion Street until it intersects with Vermillion Road (a.k. a., Co. Rd. 47). On the left you'll see a sign for Vermillion Falls Park. Find a place to park your bike and stroll through the park to the falls. Perched next to the falls is the old Gardner Flour Mill, believed to be the oldest continuing flour milling operation in Minnesota.

Half a block from the park and across the street from the Applebee's Restaurant is Las Margaritas, a family-owned Mexican restaurant known for its sizzling fajitas, tasty margaritas and efficient service.

Climb back aboard your motorcycle and continue south on Hwy. 61, which narrows to two lanes. Slow down one mile south of the edge of town and take a right on 170th Street and follow it for two miles as it becomes Kirby Avenue. The Alexis Bailly Vineyard will be on your left.

In 1978, David Bailly, a descendant of fur trader Alexis Bailly, opened the vineyard to the public after several years of experimentation with Minnesota-grown grapes. His goal was to produce wines made with French viticultural techniques. Alexis Bailly is an award-winning winery. David's daughter, Nan, is the master vintner now. Wine tastings are held Friday, Saturday and Sunday throughout the summer. Visit http://abvwines.com for hours, costs and information on special events.

If you're riding Hwy. 61 the last weekend of July, you may wish to make plans to visit the Little Log House Pioneer Village, just five miles down the road from the turnoff to the Alexis Bailly Vineyard. Take a left turn off of 61 at 220th Street and follow the signs to Steve and Sylvia Bauer's farm at 21889 Michael Blvd. You can't miss it— an entire town has sprung up in the middle of nowhere, complete with grain elevator, church, saloon and a half-scale model of the Spiral Bridge. The Bauers' hobby is to gather up and restore old buildings; their most recent acquisition was the Porky's drive-in restaurant, a long-time icon on University Avenue in St. Paul. Once a year, the Bauers open up their farm to the public for a weekend of music and an antique power show. For more information, see http://www.littleloghouseshow.com.

Back on Hwy. 61, you'll come to a stop where it intersects with MN 50, also known as "Crash Corner." You may find yourself at a bit of a disadvantage at this T, because traffic on 50 does not stop or slow down, and you will be sitting slightly below oncoming traffic. Take a good look both ways, turn left onto 50 and ride into the little town of Miesville, population 125.

Though barely a wide spot in the road, Miesville is famous for Wiederholt's Supper Club (an old-fashioned supper club), King's (54 different kinds of burgers!) and the Miesville Mudhens, the town's baseball team. If you're in luck, you can catch a Sunday afternoon ball game. Cruise through town and you'll find yourself well on the way to Red Wing.

A few miles north of Red Wing, 61 once again becomes a four-lane highway. You'll see a traditional white country church on the skyline. In front of the church and running perpendicular to Hwy. 61 is Goodhue Co. Rd. 7 (signed as Co. 7 Blvd,). Slow down and take a right, following the road as it winds toward the village of Welch. Top speed on this black-topped road is about 35 miles per hour, but you won't mind as the steep bluffs and sun-dappled forest surround you. The road twists and curves just enough to make the ride interesting.

After rounding a final curve, the road suddenly spills you into Welch, which boasts a tiny café (Trout Scream), and an even tinier post office on one side of the road, and the Cannon River Inn on the other side. The Inn is a popular stop for bikers. Trout Scream offers good, inexpensive sandwiches and ice cream. Next to the bridge that crosses the Cannon River, you'll find the old Welch mill, now the home of Welch Mill Canoeing and Tubing.

The Cannon River Inn is popular with bikers.

On the other end of the bridge, you'll come across the Cannon Valley Trail. This asphalt bicycle trail runs almost 20 miles from Cannon Falls to Red Wing. Watch out for bikers, rollerbladers and hikers!

Continue down Co. 7 Blvd. past the Welch Village Ski and Snowboard Resort to Vasa, where the main mover of the local economy appears to be Vasa Lutheran Church. It was founded by Eric Norelius, who also founded Gustavus Adolphus College in St. Peter. A small museum in Vasa celebrates the first Swedish settlements in Minnesota; it's open Sundays from May to October. Call the church office at 651-258-4327 for more information.

Co. 7 Blvd. between Welch and Vasa

A few miles more, and Co. 7 hooks up with MN 19, which you can ride east to Red Wing, or west to Cannon Falls. If you decide to go toward Red Wing, be sure to stop in at the Stoney End Music Barn, 920 Hwy. 19, just about a mile west of Hwy. 19's junction with US 61. You'll see mountain dulcimers, hand-made folk harps, banjos and Celtic instruments. Occasionally, the barn hosts bluegrass and folk music. Check www.stoneyend.com for schedules.

Red Wing is a destination in and of itself, with bars, restaurants, shopping, theater and parks, a casino, bed and breakfast establishments, antiques and great scenery. This Mississippi River town, named after a badge of office carried by a Mdewakantan Dakota chief, is often filled with bikers, especially on glorious fall weekends.

Cannon Falls, in the opposite direction, is another popular town with bikers. MN 19 from Vasa to Cannon is smooth black-top, pulling you gently through farm country. As you approach town from the east, you'll see the Cannon Falls Cemetery on your left. If you're a Civil War buff, pull into the cemetery's driveway and drive slowly to the center, where you'll find a statue of Col. William Colvill. One of the leaders of the 1st Minnesota Volunteers, Colvill and his followers were credited with helping make the Battle of Gettysburg a Union victory.

Drive further into town, and Hwy. 19 will bring you directly into the heart of Cannon Falls. Twenty-nine of the city's down-town buildings are on the National Register of Historic Sites. The Cannon Falls Chamber of Commerce offers a free walking tour guide; call 507-263-2289.

One of the hottest spots in Cannon Falls is the Cannon Valley Winery located in an old car dealership at 412 West Mill Street. The Winery's award-winning wines are produced from grapes bred by the University of Minnesota and grown locally in the nearby Sogn Valley. Hwy. 19 takes a jog to the south at 1st Street, then makes another jog to the right at Main Street. Ride Main Street to 4th Street, turn right and go one block to Mill Street. Stop in for a wine tasting, or buy some wine to take home with you. Enjoy live entertainment on weekends. Visit www.cannonriver-winery.com for hours and entertainment schedules.

After a stop at the winery, continue north on 4th Street to Minneiska Park to watch the Little Cannon River as it tumbles over the falls that give Cannon Falls its name.

Fourth Street is also Minnesota Hwy. 20. Ride north on 20 until it intersects with Hwy. 50, then take a quick left onto Hwy. 61. In downtown Hastings, you may choose to continue north on 61, or take a left onto Hwy. 55, which draws you over the Mendota Bridge and into Minneapolis.

Grand Rounds National Scenic Byway

The Grand Rounds was designated as a Minnesota State Scenic Byway in 1977 and named a National Scenic Byway in 1998. It passes through seven distinct districts within Minneapolis—the Chain of Lakes, Minnehaha, Northeast, Mississippi River, the Downtown Riverfront, Theodore Wirth and Victory Memorial. There are plenty of things to see and do along the way.

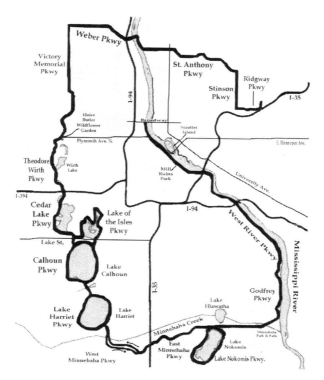

53 miles, all of them in Minneapolis

Twenty different access points allow you to jump onto the Grand Rounds almost anywhere in Minneapolis. Because of summer crowds around Lake Calhoun, we advise you to do the Grand

Rounds in April or October, when you'll have to do less crawling in traffic.

We accessed the Grand Rounds at Ridgeway Pkwy., which begins at the junction of St. Anthony Blvd. and the southeast end of Hillside Cemetery in Northeast Minneapolis. Go west on Ridgeway. It's a gentle uphill ride. The cemetery is on your right. About a half mile from the starting point, a turnout on the left offers one of the best and broadest views of the Minneapolis skyline. Get back on Ridgeway and travel westward. The parkway skirts the cemetery until you reach Stinson Blvd.

Take a right at Stinson and head north. Almost immediately, you'll reach the intersection of Stinson and Co. Rd. 88. Stay on Stinson. Ride uphill until you reach Lowry Ave. N.E. Cross Lowry and ride to St. Anthony Blvd. St. Charles Borromeo Catholic Church will be on your right. A left onto "The Boulevard" will lead you past some of Northeast's finest homes and churches.

You'll probably have to stop at the light on Johnson St. N.E. After stopping, climb west on St. Anthony Blvd. As you reach the crest of the hill, you'll see Deming Heights Park on your right. Native "Nordeasters" call it "Norwegian Hill." At 963 feet above sea level, it's the highest point in Minneapolis. Off to the left, you'll get a glimpse of the Minneapolis skyline before you make a winding descent to Central Avenue N.E.

The Minneapolis skyline from Ridgeway Parkway

Cross Central Avenue and continue along St. Anthony Blvd. Columbia Golf Course is on your right. It's a popular 18-hole course and one of the area's finest. At the southwest end of the golf course, you'll find a three-way intersection. Take a left. St. Anthony Blvd. now takes you over the Soo Railroad yards via the "Black Bridge." It's not uncommon to see train fanatics taking photos from the bridge. Ride downhill to the stoplight on Marshall St. N.E.

Cross Marshall and you'll soon see the Mississippi River on your left. St. Anthony Pkwy. ends at 37th Ave. N.E. Watch for traffic from your left coming off the Camden River Bridge. Take a left and drive over the bridge. At the west end of the bridge, take an immediate right onto Lyndale Ave. N., then move immediately into the left lane so you can turn left onto Webber Pkwy.

Webber Pond, on your right, is fed by Shingle Creek as it flows to the Mississippi. It was once a popular swimming hole. With a couple of gentle curves, Webber Pkwy. leads directly to Victory Memorial Drive.

Victory Memorial Drive is a living tribute to Hennepin County servicemen who died during World War I. Residents and school children planted many of the majestic trees that line the 3.8-mile drive. A granite memorial, dedicated in 2011, stands at its eastern entrance. "The Drive" ends at Xerxes Ave. Take a left onto Victory Memorial Pkwy. and drive south toward Theodore Wirth Pkwy., and the Chain of Lakes.

Twisting, heavily-wooded Wirth Pkwy. is a big change from spacious, open, stately Victory Memorial Pkwy. Sunlight filters through the tree canopy, and the understory has a "wild" look to it. Wirth Pkwy. actually sneaks you out of Minneapolis and into Golden Valley for just a bit as it winds through Theodore Wirth Park and its golf course, ski hill and lakes.

Although there are many places to stop along the way, two in this section really stand out: the Eloise Butler Wildflower Garden, and the Quaking Bog. Both are south of the Wirth Pkwy.-Glenwood Ave. intersection.

Founded in 1907, the Eloise Butler Wildflower Garden is the oldest wildflower garden in the United States. It was started by a Minneapolis botany teacher who wanted to preserve native wild-flowers in their habitat as the city grew around them. The 16-acre garden is divided into woodland, wetland and prairie habitats. The garden is open from April 1 to Oct. 15 from 7:30 a.m. to an hour before sunset. It's on the east side of Wirth Pkwy. as you drive south, and there is a pay parking lot.

The Quaking Bog is on the west side of the road, about two blocks south of Glenwood. There is a pay parking lot at the trail-head. Follow the signs along the switchback trails to the bog, where you'll find a floating dockway that crosses an open moat. The bog is on the other side of the moat. Because it's a delicate habitat, the Minneapolis Park and Recreation Board asks that you stay on the boardwalk. Once there, you'll find yourself surrounded by mature tamarack trees and tiny bog plants. If you go in summer, be sure to wear insect repellant.

After you've gone boghopping, get back on your bike and onto to Wirth Parkway. The road passes under I-394, and becomes Cedar Lake Pkwy. You'll cruise by Brownie Lake, said to be a great fishing hole, and along the western shores of Cedar Lake. Cedar Lake has three swimming beaches and great shore fishing. If you feel like trying another form of transportation, you can rent kayaks there and paddle from Cedar to Brownie or Lake of the Isles.

Dean Pkwy. is at the southeast end of the lake. If you go to your left, you can circumnavigate Lake of the Isles. Lake of the Isles is a man-made lake, built in the early twentieth century by dredging a small lake and a swamp. It is connected to Calhoun by a canal that passes under Lake St.

If you go to the right, you'll go to Lake Calhoun. Calhoun is by far Minneapolis' most popular lake. Summer brings out the runners, bikers, dogwalkers, inline skaters, sailboaters, windsurfers, swimmers and sunbathers. It's the place to see and be seen if you're in the twenty-something age group. If you ride this route in the summer, be prepared to "walk" your bike in some areas— it's that crowded.

Take a right from Lake St. onto Calhoun Pkwy. E. and begin your lap around the lake. With Calhoun's sparkling waters on your right, you'll see some of Minneapolis' finest homes on your left. Make a complete circle. When you get back to Lake St. and Calhoun Pkwy. E., take a right again. When you reach the southeast end of the lake, go left on William Berry Drive.

Turn right at Harriet Pkwy. W. and drive around Lake Harriet. The pace is less frenetic here, and you'll be able to enjoy more of the scenery. Stop at the Lake Harriet Bandshell for a free concert, or visit the nearby concession stand for a snack.

Or grab a ride on the Como-Harriet Streetcar. The Linden Hills station is on the corner of Lake Harriet Pkwy. and Queen Ave. S. Operated by the Minnesota Streetcar Museum, the restored antique trolley gives you a 15-minute ride for $2. The streetcar doesn't operate on rainy days, but it's otherwise open for business Monday-Friday, 6:30-8:30 p.m., and on weekends from 12:30-8:30 p.m. May-September. For exact hours, visit www.trolley-ride.org.

On Lake Harriet's east side is the Lyndale Park Rose Garden, the second oldest rose garden in the United States. More than 1,000 varieties of roses are on display. Because East Harriet Pkwy. is one-way going north, follow Rose Way Road to King's Highway. Ride south on King's Highway until it connects with Minnehaha Pkwy.

Minnehaha follows Minnehaha Creek as it meanders toward the Mississippi River. The creek, which originates in Lake Minnetonka, will sometimes be on your left and sometimes on your right as you glide down the leafy byway. You'll pass underneath I-35W as the creek cuts South Minneapolis in two.

After a stop at the semaphore on 45th St. and Cedar Ave., Minnehaha Pkwy. brings you to Lake Nokomis. Take a right on Nokomis Pkwy. W. and begin your tour. This 210-acre lake offers sailboating, canoeing and swimming beaches. The Minnesota Department of Natural Resources has stocked it with tiger muskie—a cross between Northern pike and walleye—and walleye. It's also home to several species of sunfish. There are several nice picnic areas around Nokomis, too, if you've packed a lunch.

When your circle of Nokomis is complete, you'll find yourself once again at Minnehaha Pkwy. Turn right and follow the parkway to Minnehaha Park. Stay to the right on the roundabout.

Whether you park on the street or in a lot, you'll have to pay for parking at this immensely popular park.

Minnehaha Falls

The big attraction here is Minnehaha Falls, which tumbles 53 feet as Minnehaha Creek rushes to meet the Mississippi River downstream. A few feet ahead of the falls is a small island with a statue on it. That's Hiawatha, carrying his beloved Minnehaha across the stream. Henry Wadsworth Longfellow made them—and the falls–famous in his 1855 poem, "Song of Hiawatha." Overlooking the falls is a mask of Dakota chief Little Crow by Native American artist Ed Archie Noisecat. A walking path leads you down past the falls to the Mississippi. It's been upgraded in recent years to counteract the erosion caused by more than 50,000 visitors each year.

If you're feeling hungry, visit the Sea Salt restaurant in the park pavilion. It's open from April to October. Don't be surprised if there's a line. This little eatery is very popular, but the wait is worth it. If you have time, you can rent a human-powered surrey and take a spin around the park. The nearly five-mile route takes 40 to 50 minutes. For the latest costs and hours, visit http://www.wheelfunrentals.com.

If you're anxious to get on the road again, drive out the park entrance. Stay to the right on the roundabout, then turn right on Godfrey Pkwy. Godfrey leads you under the Ford Pkwy. bridge and onto West River Pkwy.

West River Pkwy. affords you many nice views of the Mississippi River and the University of Minnesota's West Bank campus. As you pass under the Washington Ave. bridge (distinguished by the U's bold "M" painted on its side) and round a curve, you come to Bohemian Flats. This area was once an immigrant settlement that was cleared to create a river shipping port for sand and coal. It's now part of the Minneapolis parkway system. Its flat green expanse is perfect for riverboat watching.

As you continue north along the river, you'll pass under the 10th Ave. bridge and the new I-35W bridge. Built after the original freeway bridge collapsed in 2007, the bridge is lit with blue lights at night as a memorial to those who died there.

Further into downtown Minneapolis, West River Pkwy. briefly becomes First St. S. You'll pass by landmarks such as the Guthrie Theater and the Mill City Museum on the left. On the right is Mill Ruins Park where you can see what remains of the Minneapolis' west side milling district. Stop at the St. Anthony Lock and Dam to view St. Anthony Falls, once the engine of the flour-milling industry.

After you drive under the Third Ave. bridge, First St. takes on the name of West River Road. In two blocks, you'll pass under the Hennepin Ave. bridge, which connects Nicollet Island with the west bank. This is thought to be the site of the first permanent bridge across the Mississippi. The current suspension bridge was erected in 1990. Under the new bridge you'll see what looks like some kind of sculpture. They're anchorages from a previous bridge.

Just to the left of the bridge, on Nicollet Island, is the famous Grain Belt Beer sign. Although its neon outlines are not lit at night, it's still a famous Minneapolis landmark. Upstream from Nicollet Island, on the east bank, is Boom Island Park. Riverboat excursions leave here daily from May to mid-October.

West River Road takes you out of downtown, past townhouses and industrial plants. When you reach Broadway, you have a choice to make. You can ride two more blocks on West River Road to the end of the trail, or you can take a right, and cross the Broadway bridge into Northeast Minneapolis. Your tour of the Grand Rounds is ended.

What's Your Favorite Ride?

Ralph and I didn't get to ride all the roads on our list before publishing this book. We missed a few in the northeast and north central parts of the state, and I'm sure we can find more hills and curves to conquer in the southeast.

Do you have a ride that isn't covered in this book? Send me an <u>e-mail</u>, and Ralph and I will check it out. If it's "bike-worthy", we'll include it in the next edition of *Ride Minnesota*.

We would also like to include a listing of Minnesota bike clubs with a descriptive paragraph about each and a list of charitable rides, such as the Flood Run. If you're interested in including this information in the next book, please contact me at the address below.

Cynthia.sowden@gmail.com

About the Author

Cynthia Lueck Sowden was born and raised in Minneapolis. She received her bachelor's degree in journalism from the University of Minnesota and has worked in corporate communications, public relations and advertising for more than 30 years.

She began freelancing after the birth of her daughter, Elizabeth, and has written more than 100 magazine articles for various publications, including *RoadRUNNER* magazine. She is the author of two books, *Wedding Occasions: 101 New Party Themes for Wedding Showers, Rehearsal Dinners, Engagement Parties and More!* and *An Anniversary to Remember: Celebrations for the Years One to Seventy-Five.* She also contributed chapters to *Masters of Sales* by Ivan Misner and Don Morgan, and *How I Got the Gig*, edited by Susan Carter.

Ralph Sowden is an electrical engineer who caught the motorcycle bug when he got his grandfather's Suzuki B100P running again and took it for a test drive. The couple lives in Minneapolis.

List of Maps

Index

Made in the USA
Lexington, KY
04 May 2013